Haunted
Northern
California

Ghosts and Strange Phenomena
the Golden State

Charles A. Stansfield Jr.

Illustrations by Heather Adel Wiggins

STACKPOLE
BOOKS

For Diane, my one and only, the light of my life—
a wonderful wife, superb mother,
and most generous grandmother

Copyright © 2009 by Stackpole Books

Published by
STACKPOLE BOOKS
5067 Ritter Road
Mechanicsburg, PA 17055
www.stackpolebooks.com

Printed in the United States of America

10 9 8 7 6 5 4 3 2 1

FIRST EDITION

Design by Beth Oberholtzer
Cover design by Tessa J. Sweigert

Library of Congress Cataloging-in-Publication Data

Stansfield, Charles A.
    Haunted northern California : ghosts and strange phenomena of the Golden State / Charles A. Stansfield, Jr.—1st ed.
        p.   cm.
    Includes bibliographical references.
    ISBN-13: 978-0-8117-3586-5 (pbk.)
    ISBN-10: 0-8117-3586-9 (pbk.)
    1. Ghosts—California, Northern. 2. Haunted places—California, Northern.
I. Title.
BF1472.U6S73   2009
133.109794—dc22

                                                            2009003157

Contents

Contents

Introduction

GHOSTS ARE ALL AROUND US, OR SO IT WOULD SEEM. RECENT SURVEYS indicate that about half of Americans either claim to have had a direct experience with the supernatural or have relatives or friends who sincerely believe they've had encounters with ghosts, witches, vampires, or monsters. Add in the scores of millions who've witnessed UFOs and you have a clear majority of believers, or at least open-minded skeptics.

Contemporary Americans are not alone in their fascination with the supernatural. People always have expressed interest, if not total belief, in ghosts and goblins. Consider what has happened to Halloween in America over the years. What was once pretty much a children's holiday, an excuse for the kids to dress up in costumes and gorge on candy for one evening, has become an occasion for ever more elaborate decorations on houses and lawns. Fake tombstones with witty epitaphs sprout from suburban lawns. Imitation cobwebs festoon trees, and orange twinkle lights join jack-o'-lanterns in windows. Stores even sell a variety of greeting cards for the occasion, right down to "Happy Halloween from my dog to your dog." It is no coincidence that ghosts, witches, vampires, and monsters of all types are enduringly favorite Halloween costumes for both children and adults.

Interest in the supernatural seems to be universal. Every human society that we know of has had traditions of ghosts, witches, and monsters. As fans of Dracula movies know, tales from Eastern Europe feature vampires transforming from humans into wolves or bats, known as shape-shifting. More than seven thousand miles away, in the southwestern deserts of America, the Navajo believe that witches can metamorphose from human form into wolves or owls. Is it pure coincidence that people of such different cultures, religions, languages, and races just happen to have almost identical legends?

In the ancient African kingdom of Ethiopia, it was customary for people to carry a fetish bag filled with small natural or handmade objects believed to have magical powers to protect them against evil spirits. Many Native American tribes also had the habit of carrying pouches filled with small quantities of magical herbs, plant pollen, and oddly shaped or colored pebbles to ward off witches and bad luck.

Belief in witches was so strong in Europe four and five centuries ago that scores of thousands of people were convicted of witchcraft and either hanged or burned alive. In England alone, thirty thousand people were killed because their neighbors thought they were witches. House cats were thought to be familiars, feline "henchmen" of human witches and in league with Satan. In an orgy of senseless violence, hundreds of thousands of cats were killed throughout Europe. Ironically, this led to a huge increase in rat populations, which helped spread the dreaded black death—bubonic plague. On the other side of the world, Japanese folklore contains stories of ghostly vampire cats—a truly fearsome combination of supernatural threats.

Legends about monsters, both in the sea and on land, abound in every culture. Are they just legends, or could there be truth at the roots of these stories? For many centuries, sailors told about fantastic sea monsters whose many flailing arms were lined with suction cups, creatures equipped with huge, sharp beaks capable of tearing men apart. Were these just tall tales growing out of ignorance and isolation and fueled by rum? Such stories were once dismissed as impossible by scientists. How could there exist such animals, capable of attacking whales? But now we have abundant evidence that, yes, giant deep-sea squid more than thirty feet long are real.

Could Bigfoot actually exist? Native American legends say yes, as do the scores of people living in the Pacific Northwest who claim to have seen the creature. About 150 years ago, in the rainforests of central Africa, the locals told stories about the "men of the forest"— great, hairy, manlike animals that were more powerful than humans. They were at the same time shy and curious about people and were pretty smart. Scientists classified these tales as mere folk-lore—until they finally came face-to-face with gorillas. Could an apelike animal live in places like Northern California? Why not? We now know that the great apes are not strictly vegetarians, as once assumed. They've been seen hunting and eating monkeys, as well as termites and other insects. They, like people, can consume a wide variety of food, both plant and animal. If they did live in the forests of the great Northwest, they would be able to find enough food. It has been observed that although most animal species may have originated in the tropics, many have successfully migrated to cooler climates. These animals even get larger in size the farther from the equator, as greater body bulk becomes a survival advantage. Siberian tigers and Alaskan Kodiak bears, for example, are larger than their cousins to the south.

So just because we don't see a Bigfoot in a museum or zoo yet doesn't mean it doesn't exist. There are still mysteries out there.

For believers and skeptics alike, any encounter with ghosts is not to be taken lightly. Even those who very seriously doubt the existence of ghosts express fear of them. Our fascination with ghosts, strongly evident in all forms of the media, is likely related to our deep-seated fears that the dead might return in spirit to harass us or do us harm. Consider the pyramids of ancient Egypt— the largest stone structures on earth. They were built to protect and preserve the bodies of dead kings so that they could succeed in traveling to the world of the spirits. The living went to great lengths to help the dead move on and not stay to haunt the living. Fear of ghosts built the pyramids.

Nine thousand miles west of Egypt, some Indian tribes living in the Colorado River Valley customarily destroyed or discarded all the personal possessions of the deceased, such as clothing, jewelry, and tools. This was done out of the belief that the spirits of the dead would remain to haunt the living who dared take over the dead person's possessions.

Ghost stories are both common and popular because they are a way of exploring the nature of life and death—a very serious, even disturbing question that we are uneasy confronting. Does some form of existence continue after the death of a body? Are we, in some way, immortal? Can the spirits of the dead somehow cross the barrier between the living and the dead?

Perhaps the gentle mocking of death at Halloween is a safety valve to diminish our fears about the end of life. We can joke about serious and complex concerns that we have by dressing up as ghosts and thus reducing their mystery.

Where do you stand on the subject of ghosts and other supernatural phenomena? Are you a true believer, a confirmed skeptic, or part of that large crowd of people who are just not sure? One way or another, you can enjoy a good story even if you don't quite accept the supernatural aspect of the tale as probable truth.

You are about to embark on a voyage of discovery, a survey of Northern California's dark side, its hidden world of ghosts, monsters, witches, and devils. The stories are organized geographically into five regions: San Francisco and the Pacific Coast southward to Carmel; the East Bay portion of the San Francisco metropolitan area, including the Santa Clara Valley; the Sacramento Valley, including the state capital; the coast northward from the Golden Gate to the Oregon border; and the Northern Sierra and the desert country along the Nevada border. Enjoy your tour of the spooky and supernatural side of this part of the Golden State.

San Francisco and the Central Coast

IN ADDITION TO SAN FRANCISCO, ONE OF THE GREATEST CITIES IN THE world, this relatively small region includes the Pacific Coast southward to Monterey and Carmel, some of the loveliest real estate on Earth. The fabled city by the bay hosts a variety of ghosts that are both interesting and cosmopolitan: the spirit of a very protective first lady, an elegant phantom, the specter of one of America's most frightening baby killers, a ghost who wants to play cards, and a phantom who will lovingly tuck you into bed. There's also a haunted golf course, and Alcatraz Island is believed to still imprison several spirits. Farther down the coast, you might encounter the ghost of a Spanish padre, a phantom willing to peacefully coexist with the living, and the spirits of some revolutionary Mexicans.

The Ghost in the Machine

People who use copy machines regularly as part of their jobs have wondered on occasion if the copier was possessed by a malignant spirit or demon. Some offices post comic "notices" near the copier advising: "This machine is equipped with a special sensor that picks up any urgency on your part. It will malfunction in direct proportion to how big a rush you might be in." This note becomes progressively less funny if, indeed, some electronic gremlin causes a breakdown during an important job at 4:30 P.M. on a Friday.

If many people have considered, however briefly, the likelihood that copy machines can be possessed by an evil spirit, how about one really controlled by a ghost? A group of office workers in a downtown San Francisco skyscraper are convinced that a copy machine there contains the spirit of a recently deceased coworker.

For more than three decades, Miss Mayer was a fixture in the office. Only special close friends called her by her first name, Sophie, or even knew her first name, as she was a very private person. Miss Mayer had never married nor, as far as anyone knew, ever had any romantic attachments. She was "married to her job," as her friends put it. Her public image was that of a prim and proper spinster, but she sometimes revealed an impish sense of humor.

Miss Mayer was in charge of the copying room. She ruled her little domain like a medieval monarch, seldom brooking any breaks in her routine. Heaven help anyone who thought that he or she could use the copier. Miss Mayer would point out, correctly, that the frequency of machine malfunctions and breakdowns increased in proportion to the number of different users. Then, too, it seemed that the copier ran jobs smoothly and error-free when its mistress was at the controls, almost as though it sensed her calm, steady hand and responded like a well-trained dog.

Mayer's contentment came to a sad and sudden end when a new vice president of the company showed up, determined to juice up his résumé by cutting costs. He ended the custom of Christmas bonuses and replaced the formerly excellent health insurance with a third-rate HMO.

This abrupt decline in the quality of medical care had tragic consequences for Miss Mayer. The penny-pinching new policy decreed that at her age, mammograms no longer were necessary and would not be reimbursed, nor would annual pelvic exams. Miss Mayer's breast cancer was not detected until it had advanced to a fatal stage. An inept surgeon in an unsanitary old hospital sealed Miss Mayer's fate. She was overwhelmed by a staph infection that she had contracted in the hospital.

Two coworkers and close friends determined to carry out Miss Mayer's most unorthodox and, indeed, bizarre last request, communicated from her deathbed. They secretly scattered a small quantity of her cremated ashes in the copier room, right behind the copy machine. Given that the notorious vice president had cut the maintenance and janitorial staff in half, it was a good bet that the ashes would be there for a long while. The balance of Miss Mayer's ashes were scattered equally illegally in her favorite place, Muir Woods National Monument.

Then the copier meltdown occurred. With multiple users now, and in the absence of Miss Mayer's stern supervision, the rate of machine malfunctions escalated. It didn't help that in yet another cost-cutting move, the vice president unwisely had canceled the copier's maintenance and repair contract. Mysteriously, the machine refused to function at all for a week following Miss Mayer's death. The day that the ashes were surreptitiously deposited behind the copier, it ran off a thousand copies of Miss Mayer's memo concerning submitting all copying requests to her with twenty-four hours' notice. No one had programmed it to do that. Then, in a typical last-minute rush, the machine had been given the task of copying and stapling a lengthy report from the vice president on increasing office efficiency. The machine made the copies all right, but then stapled them on all four sides of the pages.

One morning, the first user of the machine found that it had made multiple copies of a memo from the vice president to all employees, announcing a day off with pay to those wishing to attend or participate in a run through Golden Gate Park to benefit a breast cancer charity. Most office staff had already left before the irate vice president could deny authorizing any such thing.

The most outrageous and, it turned out, final copying job for the machine was a memo, which everyone denied writing or putting in the copier, concerning the untimely death of the vice president. The memo advised all employees that they would be paid for the day when the office closed to commemorate his passing. When this was brought to the attention of the very much alive vice president, he flew into a rage and marched into the copying room. Reaching behind the machine to unplug it, he was electrocuted by a loose high-voltage connection.

Everyone enjoyed the paid day off promised by that last memo. Incidentally, the memo was signed by Miss Mayer.

The Shivering Spirit

A beautiful old mansion now converted into a restaurant in San Francisco was haunted for a time by a shivering spirit. The present owners have asked that the property not be identified, for reasons that will become obvious.

The house was built a few years after the great earthquake of 1906. After five decades as a family home, it was reincarnated as an elegant, intimate restaurant, as famous for its ambience as for its food. Things were going well when a young man whom we'll call Jack entered the picture. Some say that Jack was picked up in a bar by the then-owner, who had a passion for attractive young men as well as exotic European sports cars and gourmet food.

Jack soon displayed a flair for cooking in addition to his personal charms. He learned quickly and was by now a permanent resident, happily helping out in the kitchen and generally making himself useful. He seems to have had no fixed address before meeting the restaurant proprietor; the presumption was that he was a runaway, a drifter. Despite his yearlong stay in the old house, no one even knew his last name.

Eventually the relationship soured. It was rumored among the restaurant staff that Jack was pushing for part ownership of the profitable establishment. The owner, whom we'll call George, adamantly refused. Jack moved out of the master bedroom into a third-floor guest room. George and Jack began bickering in front of staff and guests. Violent flare-ups became a regular feature of closing time, when it was George's habit to have a few stiff drinks while supervising Jack's cleanup efforts.

Suddenly one day, Jack was gone. There was no comment at all from George.

Within a week of his mysterious disappearance, however, Jack was back—sort of. When employees showed up one morning to begin the day's food preparation, they found the lights on and sauces bubbling away on the stove. Pots and pans left to soak the night before had been scoured and put away. Freshly chopped vegetables were found bagged in the refrigerator. These chores had all been Jack's responsibilities. There was one other odd thing—there were puddles of salt water on the floor.

After a few weeks of the unseen kitchen helper's efforts, Jack appeared in person, sitting wearily on a chair. He was a bluish-white, misty figure, nude and shivering with cold. He was soaking wet, with bits of seaweed tangled in his hair. "I'm cold, very cold," he said. "Can you get me warm clothes?" A very apprehensive worker went up to the bedrooms and gathered up some of George's clothes, cautiously handing them over to the trembling image. Once warmed up, Jack's spirit seemed to just evaporate. The suspicion grew that George, who was known for his violent temper, had killed Jackie in an alcoholic rage and dumped the body in the bay. The shivering ghost is alleged to have made several more visits to the kitchen while George was present, causing the owner to run ashen-faced out of the room. After a few months of encounters with the nude, trembling, cold lad, George committed suicide. No one again saw Jack's ghost, although on occasion, dirty pots and pans left in the sink somehow ended up clean and bright the next morning.

The Shade of the Emperor

If you are out on the streets of downtown San Francisco on a cool and foggy evening, you've had more than a few drinks, and you are very lucky, you just might get to meet an emperor, or at least his ghost. This engaging phantom will be wearing an elaborate uniform, dripping with gold braid. Rows of ornate medals decorate the coat. An elaborately engraved sword hangs at his side. You have caught a fleeting glimpse of Norton the First, emperor of the United States and protector of Mexico.

You didn't know that the United States had an emperor? Well, San Franciscans back in the 1860s and 1870s not only acknowledged the Emperor Norton, but they saluted him and paid "taxes" to him as well. Norton surely was the most beloved emperor the United States never had.

Emperor Norton was quite insane, but his insanity was no threat to anyone. His madness was of a benevolent sort, and San Franciscans were entertained by his antics. Joshua A. Norton was born in England in 1819 and came to San Francisco in 1849 at the age of thirty. A shrewd speculator, he arrived with $40,000 in cash, which he soon increased to $250,000. He bought and sold real estate,

ships, and mining claims, pyramiding his wealth. But when he and some associates tried to corner the rice market, his gamble failed. Norton lost it all—his real estate, his ships, his mining claims, his cash, and sadly, his mind.

Mentally, he couldn't cope with going from great wealth to poverty, and he became deluded that he had been elected emperor. He charmed a tailor into making him a fantastic uniform and paraded around the streets accompanied by two mongrel dogs, Bummer and Lazarus. He issued a series of imperial decrees and proclamations, some of them quite funny and some truly visionary. For example, he ordered the building of a bridge across the Golden Gate, a truly remarkable plan and something that didn't happen until 1937. One of his most popular decrees dissolved both the Democratic and Republican parties "in the interests of peace and harmony among all men." Restaurants provided him with free meals, as his presence attracted paying customers. He sold hand-printed "imperial bonds" for 50 cents, which his "subjects" cheerfully bought. Saloons across the city paid him "taxes" in the form of free drinks. He wrote checks for 50 cents, which all banks honored. As emperors go, Norton the First was a benevolent and beloved figure. When he died on the street in 1880, San Francisco gave him a great send-off. Should you happen to see the emperor's ghost, remember to bow slightly to receive his smiling salute in return. We never had a kinder, more harmless ruler.

A Most Elegant Ghost

The shimmering, almost transparent figure walks slowly down the staircase of a beautiful mansion. A phosphorescent glow outlines the form of a late-middle-aged, very handsome man. Dressed in an elegant tuxedo, complete with a silk embroidered waistcoat, the ghost appears to be wearing diamond cufflinks and an impressive diamond ring. Oddly, the tuxedo is dripping salt water, and long strands of seaweed cling to the phantom's hair and coat. His face is frozen in a rather haughty welcoming smile. Just as the observer is about to speak, the ghost disappears in a swirl of mist. This is a most elegant ghost, which is fitting, as it is the spirit of a man who much enjoyed being described as "a most elegant man."

This ghost, which makes regular appearances in what is now the main building of Notre Dame de Namur University in San Mateo, is alleged to be that of William Chapman Ralston. The college, located on Ralston Avenue in San Mateo, was once the home of Ralston, who led a flamboyant life and died a mysterious death.

Ralston called his mansion Belmont, derived from the French phrase for "beautiful mountain." He had purchased a charming villa from one Count Cipriani and immediately set about enlarging it. The mansion was expanded from rooms for 30 guests to accommodations for 120. The floors were redone in parquetry and the walls paneled in mirrors in the style of Versailles. Carpets, drapes, chandeliers, and furniture were imported from France, Italy, and China. Outbuildings contained greenhouses, a bowling alley, and a gymnasium. A separate house was built for the Chinese domestic staff. The stables for Ralston's thoroughbred horses were paneled in mahogany. Ralston built his own gasworks on the estate to provide brilliant lights for his home. To irrigate his extensive formal garden, a dam and reservoir were built in the nearby hills.

Ralston liked nothing better than to throw fabulous parties, inviting hundreds of guests to meet rich and famous personages such as Mark Twain. William Chapman Ralston regarded himself as American royalty and was determined to live in an appropriately grand style. He had made a vast fortune with his interests in the fabulous Comstock Mine, which produced silver by the ton. Ralston founded the Bank of California, one of the largest in the state. Unfortunately, he recklessly speculated with the bank's funds. The bank, and Ralston, lost so much money that it closed its doors on August 26, 1875. The bank's collapse caused a financial panic throughout the state. The following day, Ralston's body was found floating in the bay. It was never determined whether it was a suicide or murder. Certainly, many depositors and employees had good reason to kill the man whose lack of judgment and greed had ruined them. Ralston's fabulous mansion became a private insane asylum for a while before being taken over by the Sisters of Notre Dame de Namur, who opened their college in 1926.

The most elegant ghost of a most elegant man still descends the great staircase to welcome his guests, just as he liked to do in life. You need have no fear of his ghost—it disappears in an instant after sensing a living being in its house.

Don't Disturb the President

San Francisco's Palace Hotel is a well-known landmark just east of Union Square at Market and New Montgomery streets. This grand hotel has an interesting history. The original structure was destroyed by fire in the 1906 earthquake. According to legend, the present building was completed in 1909 using the salvaged steel frame of the original. The beautifully restored Palace offers all the amenities a contemporary guest could wish for, and its more than five hundred units are renowned for their peaceful luxury. Not only is the sound insulation quite effective, but staff and guests alike have been admonished to be quiet by a very determined ghost.

The experience of a recent guest is typical. She was walking down the corridor on the eighth floor with her admittedly rambunctious youngster in tow. Suddenly a very stern-looking woman in her sixties appeared. She was wearing a dress draped in beads of the style popular in the 1920s. Her hair was styled in tight waves. Steel-rimmed glasses framed her fiercely glaring eyes. A thrusting jaw and beaklike nose completed her aggressive persona. "Quiet!" she demanded. "The president is resting!" "The president of what?" asked the impudent little boy. "The president of the United States!" was the rejoinder. Duly impressed, mother and child tiptoed quietly to the elevator. When the guest asked a bellboy when the president had arrived at the Palace, she was met with a blank stare. "What president?" he asked. "We don't have the president here now." The guest later was informed by a friendly chambermaid that her encounter was not all that unusual. "Oh, that's just Mrs. Harding's ghost—we see her whenever there's noise in the halls."

Florence Kling DeWolfe Harding was, like her ghost, strong-willed and outspoken. In the contemporary age of intense and intrusive press scrutiny of political candidates and their families, Florence's lurid past, if revealed, could have kept her husband out of the White House. Florence had an illegitimate child with another man before she wed future president Warren G. Harding. Her son's father never married her, and the son died at age thirty-five from alcoholism and tuberculosis, alone and in poverty, far from the glamour of the White House.

Mrs. Harding was a very assertive first lady who was fiercely protective of her husband, as well as aggressively ambitious for him. President Warren Harding died suddenly, and some say mysteriously, at the Palace Hotel on August 2, 1923. The exact cause of death is not known, as Mrs. Harding forbade an autopsy, and no one, including new president Calvin Coolidge, had the nerve to override her decision. At the time, there were suspicions that Mrs. Harding had poisoned her husband. Her supposed motive was to spare him the disgrace and possible impeachment that could have followed when the many scandals of his corrupt and inept administration came to light.

Was the iron-willed first lady a murderer? We'll never know. Florence Harding died on August 4, 1924, exactly a year and two days after her husband.

But her spirit, it is claimed, still appears to protect his peaceful privacy. "Quiet!" orders the phantom. "Don't disturb the president." And you'd better listen.

The Ghost of a True Gentleman

Few today know the reason for the twin granite shafts positioned at the southern tip of Lake Merced in the southwestern part of San Francisco. One stone bears the name "Terry" in bronze letters; the other is labeled "Broderick." On foggy mornings, particularly in the fall, a ghostly figure has been seen at the first site, firing an old-fashioned pistol into the ground, then clutching his own breast in a spasm of agony, followed by his collapse. Too bad this phantom never speaks, for his is an interesting story.

This ghost is said to be that of U.S. Senator David C. Broderick, who was fatally wounded on this spot in a duel with California's Supreme Court Chief Justice David S. Terry. Their duel was the product of a long, bitter struggle within the state's Democratic party over the leading issue of the day—slavery.

Chief Justice Terry was a leading supporter of the southern viewpoint that human slavery was necessary and justifiable. He was a Kentucky-born aristocrat whose family had prospered on the sweat of their slaves. He considered himself a cultured, educated gentleman; he probably never worked up a sweat in his life. Broderick, in contrast, was the son of an Irish stonemason. Broderick lacked the fine clothes and fancy manners of Terry. David Broderick learned politics in the rough-and-tumble world of New York City's Tammany Hall. He was a friend of the eminent orator and activist African American leader Frederick Douglass and was ardently antislavery in his views.

Justice Terry attacked David Broderick for socializing with African Americans and for advocating freeing all slaves, by force if necessary. Broderick stood up for himself and his cause, using the plain language of the streets and questioning Terry's judgment, ethics, and ancestry.

Terry challenged Broderick to a duel. Broderick knew he'd be mocked as a coward if he refused, so he accepted, though duels were illegal. At dawn on September 13, 1859, the two men stood thirty paces apart. Broderick fired first. He deliberately fired his bullet into the ground, which was often done in duels to avoid hitting one's opponent while at the same time proving one was not a coward. Terry, in contrast, then aimed for Broderick's heart and fatally wounded him, although he easily could have followed the other man's honorable example.

It was reported that thirty thousand people crowded into Portsmouth Square to hear the funeral oration. Who was the real gentleman: the senator who deliberately wasted his only bullet or the judge who callously shot a defenseless man? Within eighteen months, the nation would be in a Civil War to decide the issue of slavery.

Some say that Broderick is still standing up for racial equality. His ghost reportedly joins civil rights demonstrations, marching to demonstrate his continued commitment to this noble cause.

The Shades of Alcatraz

The local Maidu Indians believed that the island was cursed, inhabited by evil spirits that would attack, even kill, any mortals foolish enough to set foot there. Certainly, most of the men confined there cursed the day they first came to Alcatraz.

Spanish explorers discovered the island in 1545 and named it Alcatraz, meaning "pelican." The 22-acre island is quite rugged, with most of its area lying between 62 and 136 feet above the sea. Large waves and strong currents make landing on the island a dicey proposition, and cold fogs make it an unpleasant, inhospitable site.

Other than name it, the Spanish did little with the island. After the American takeover of California, the new governor gave Alcatraz to a buddy, who then sold it to the federal government, which wanted it as the site of a fortress to defend San Francisco from any enemy fleet. The feds built a lighthouse and spent $2 million on fortifications. It was in use as a military prison by 1868 and housed rebellious Indian leaders as well. Alcatraz seemed made for its long-time role as a prison. It was isolated by surrounding brutally cold, swirling, unpredictable ocean currents. The island was not remote, only a twenty-minute boat ride from San Francisco. After the 1906 earthquake demolished the walls of San Francisco's city prison, its inmates were transferred to Alcatraz. When America was terrorized by a crime wave of bank robberies and general mayhem in the early 1930s, the federal government took over Alcatraz as a new escape-proof prison. Notorious gangsters such as Al Capone, Alvin Karpis, "Machine Gun" Kelly, and Robert "Birdman" Stroud did hard time on "The Rock." From 1934 to its closure in 1963, Alcatraz housed more than fifteen hundred of America's most infamous and dangerous prisoners.

Many prisoners left the island in coffins. Those who left alive carried a heavy load of bitterness, resentment, and hatred. It is said that Alcatraz today contains many ghosts, that many spirits haunt this National Park Service historic site.

Warden Johnston, the onetime federal prison's most famous— or maybe infamous—chief, is said to remain in his office, at least in spirit. There are those who claim that mixed into the sounds of waves crashing on the rocks, the wind howling around the prison's empty halls, and the raucous cries of seagulls can be heard the warden over the loudspeaker system: "Stay in line! Stay two feet away from anyone else! Do not speak! Eyes forward, hands at your side!" The barked orders echo faintly over the decades and seem to blend with the moaning wind.

The sounds of a woman sobbing have been heard in the visitors' room. During one Christmas party for the National Park Service staff, a figure dressed as a prison guard made a brief but memorable appearance. Apparently very unhappy at hearing the sounds of merriment in the old prison, the grim-faced phantom guard marched into the party and calmly poured what appeared to be a bucket of blood into the punch bowl. Needless to say, the party came to an abrupt end, as he doubtless intended. Cries and moans frequently come from the notorious Cell Block D—the "treatment unit," which prisoners used to call "Hellcatraz."

On especially foggy nights, the long-defunct lighthouse again shines its beam out to sea, despite a lack of electricity. The eeriest and most common phantom is simply called "the Thing" by old-timers on the staff. The Thing is a disembodied set of red glowing eyes that stare hypnotically from darkened cells or corridors, then blink and disappear. No one is sure just who or what the Thing might be, but no one is about to approach it to investigate.

Enjoy your visit to Alcatraz, and don't miss the last boat.

She Can't Wash It Away

The phantom of a rather stout, late-middle-aged woman is at the same time frightening and saddening. She is wearing a bloodstained white apron over a flowered dress. Atop her head, her graying hair is piled in an old-fashioned bun. Her expression is one of anguish and regret. Her lips move soundlessly. She is washing bloody hands in an old, white-enameled tin basin that hovers, without visible support, in front of her at waist level. It is filled with blood. As the ghostly figure slowly advances, the basin precedes her.

This intriguing ghost is said to haunt the basement of an old building on Maiden Lane. The present owners prefer that the exact address not be revealed. Whether the street's name was selected intentionally as an ironic reference to its history is not known, but it was once called Morton Street and was part of the notorious Barbary Coast district, a wide-open red-light area catering to sailors, transients, prostitutes, and criminals of all types. Morton Street at that time was lined with bordellos; it can be assumed that maidens were scarce on the future Maiden Lane. The Barbary Coast flourished from the late nineteenth century until 1917, when the city ended its tolerance of brothels, gambling houses, and predatory bars.

It is widely believed that the hand-washing ghost is that of a well-known character from the heyday of the Barbary Coast—a person known as Aunt Bessie. Aunt Bessie supposedly had been a prostitute who worked her way up to becoming a madam, and then moved on to a later career as an abortionist. The prostitution trade produced a need for an abortionist, and Aunt Bessie was much in demand. Aunt Bessie always claimed that many women who came to her for abortions were respectable married women from much better neighborhoods.

Many regard abortion as the cold-blooded murder of the innocent. Apparently Aunt Bessie has come to agree with this viewpoint, for her ghost walks in remorse for past sins. A deaf man, on seeing the ghost once, read the phantom's lips as lamenting, "I'm sorry, oh so sorry. Please forgive me."

And thus Aunt Bessie's spirit still stalks the dingy basement where she once practiced her evil trade, bemoaning her termination of so many pregnancies. Her ghost, in its guilty anxiety, has been able to command the basin to hover before her as she futilely attempts to wash the blood from her hands. Her hands will never be clean, and her conscience never clear, so beware the ghost of Aunt Bessie. She is stained forever with the blood of the innocent that she can't wash away.

Imprisoned Spirits

Jails are common "hot spots" in the world of spirits. It is said that unhappy, tormented souls are among those most likely to become ghosts upon death, as they are too restless or motivated by vengeance to move on to the next plane of existence. The psychological trauma of being in prison might scar the soul, leading to an angrily confused spirit remaining in the jail cell or grim corridors of their incarceration.

The old Monterey Jail is said to be haunted by at least three malevolent spirits. The building no longer functions as a jail and is open to the public. The sand-colored stone structure was erected in 1854 and once housed such infamous prisoners as Tiburcio Vasquez, the "gentleman bandit"; the notorious killer Anastacia Garcia; and Matt Tarpey, who was lynched by vigilantes for his cold-blooded murder of a beautiful young woman. Many claim to have encountered the ghosts of these three criminals, along with the phantoms of innumerable highwaymen, thieves, and con men from the old days.

The murderous bandit Tiburcio Vasquez terrorized coastal California between 1854, when he began his criminal career by stabbing a constable, and 1875, when he was hanged at San Jose. Vasquez liked to think of himself as a gentleman bandit, one who robbed with flair and could kill with a smile on his lips. He was, he claimed, "muy caballero"—very gentlemanly. He cultivated an image as a kind of Robin Hood and charmed his way out of jail numerous times before he outraged the public by committing a senseless atrocity. During a robbery, he shot and killed three men in a particularly brutal fashion. One victim was a deaf man who had not obeyed Vasquez's orders because he hadn't heard them. Another was a Portuguese who couldn't understand the bandit's commands, and a third was a hotel keeper who happened to be standing behind a door when the bandit fired a bullet into it.

It is said that Tiburcio Vasquez's ghost strolls nonchalantly along the corridors, twirling a six-gun in his hand. The phantom smiles at his potential victim and politely requests that his wallet and watch be handed over. If refused, the phantom aims his weapon, but then evaporates into thin air. Several visitors have reportedly been quite unnerved by this experience with a supernatural thug.

Others have seen a small cloud of mist slowly resolve itself into the faintly glowing image of a man in one of the cells. The figure is earnestly reading a Bible while wearing a hangman's noose of thick, yellow rope. This ghost has to be that of Anastacia Garcia, a one-time inmate who had been convicted of murder. The sheriff had promised Garcia that he was going to send him to meet God, neglecting to mention that he was going to send him on his final journey at the end of a stout rope.

A third ghost in the old Monterey Jail is that of an obviously terrified man who attempts to hide from everyone, but not very successfully. The phantom cowers in corners, trying to be invisible, but the loud pounding of his heart gives him away. His guilty heart sounds like a hammer hitting an anvil. This ghost is that of Matt Tarpey, who didn't get to enjoy the jail's hospitality for long. Tarpey was accused of the rape and murder of a young girl, slicing open his victim and removing her organs, a particularly gruesome crime foreshadowing the later exploits of London's Jack the Ripper. An enraged mob invaded the jail and hanged Matt Tarpey from the nearest tree. The sheriff made no attempt to stop this example of rough justice. It is said that Tarpey's body was left hanging from the tree so that vultures could "tear him open and feast on his innards," as they said at the time.

Show Reverence or Else!

It is possible, at least according to a few, that a long-dead priest might occasionally encourage the skeptical, profane, and unrepentant to kneel respectfully in church. Or is this story just one of an uneven sanctuary floor? Perhaps it all depends on whether you believe that the unseen spirit of Father Junipero Serra could raise the stone covering his grave just enough to trip disrespectful visitors.

Father Serra was a very important figure in early California history. He first arrived here in 1768, after the king of Spain had decided that if his country didn't seriously enforce its claims to California with permanent settlement, British and Russian adventurers might take it away. Spanish control was to be established by both missions and presidios, or military posts.

In 1769, Father Serra established Mission San Diego, followed by a mission at Monterey in 1770. That second mission, of twenty-one that eventually would be built, was moved to Carmel the next year and reestablished as Mission San Carlos Borromeo del Rio Carmelo. Father Junipero Serra had been appointed *padre-presidente* ("father-president") of California and assigned to oversee all missions in the colony.

Serra's presidency seems to have reflected his energy, organizational ability, and devotion to his cause. Reportedly, he did not suffer fools gladly and could come down hard on the slothful or the disrespectful—supporting the notion that his spirit may continue to respond to such transgressions to this day.

The mission at Carmel became Father Serra's headquarters. When he died in 1784, he was buried beneath the sanctuary floor in front of the altar. After 1833, when the Mexican Congress decreed the secularization of all the missions, Mission San Carlos fell on hard times. Its Indians, no longer bound by law to work and live there, drifted away. Although the five-foot-thick stone walls remained, the shingled roof collapsed, and the church was abandoned. That was when the mystery of the tilted pavement stone began.

As the legend goes, sometime in the 1860s, a curious visitor entered the ruined church, possibly looking for some artifacts to steal. As he approached the altar, he suddenly tripped on the slightly raised edge of a paving stone. Smack! Abruptly he found himself on his knees before the altar, a position he definitely hadn't anticipated or desired. A minor accident, or was it really accidental?

Over time, a pattern became apparent. Although the stone floor of the sanctuary appeared to be perfectly smooth and even, casual visitors repeatedly tripped over the stone atop Father Serra's final resting place, putting them unwillingly on their knees. Was the good Father's spirit at work, ensuring that anyone approaching the altar without proper reverence would pitch forward on his or her knees?

Even after the restoration of the Carmel Mission in the 1880s, the mystery of the "tripping stone" continued. The mission church hosts many tourists, some of whom seem to be too casual about considering the religious significance of the church in addition to its obvious historical importance. Splat! Down they go, landing hard on their knees. The "tripping stone" lies perfectly flat and even; it couldn't have tripped them. Or could it? When visiting the Mission San Carlos Borromeo del Rio Carmelo, remember to have a properly reverent attitude—and watch your step around Father Serra's grave.

Dealing with a Ghost

Carmel by the Sea, better known as just Carmel, is different, really different, by design and is kept that way by tough zoning ordinances. Its residents like to call it "the Village," and many movie stars have joined the artists, writers, and scientists who settled here. Even the ghosts are different, judging by one family's recent experience.

Carmel was founded as an artists' colony in 1904, and its residents have tried hard to maintain its informal village atmosphere. Real estate values are impressively high, and houses seldom change hands, so the mere fact that a house is found to be haunted doesn't necessarily mean that the occupants would decide to move on. Leave Carmel just because a ghost is in residence? Not on your life. It seems that some folks would rather make a deal with the ghost.

The ghost manifested soon after the Johnson family (not their real name) moved in. As often happens in these cases, the family pets were the first to sense a supernatural presence. Puss the cat, when introduced to her new home, thoroughly explored every nook, as cats will. When she entered the master bedroom, however, she became noticeably agitated. She began to growl, the fur along her spine rose stiffly, and her tail twitched. Suddenly Puss yowled as though in pain, and with ears flattened and eyes wide, she bolted from the room. Puss refused to enter that room ever again.

Laddie, the Johnsons' amiable, laid-back yellow Lab, slowly, cautiously entered the same room but then turned tail, yelping as though kicked, and ran from the room. He, too, avoided that room ever afterward. The family's ten-year-old son swore that he saw the figure of an old man standing by the closet in the master bedroom. When challenged by the boy, the figure faded away. The couple's first night in the master bedroom took on a nightmarish quality. When they turned out the lights, preparing for sleep, they noticed a faint greenish glow in a far corner of the room. Gradually, the glowing mist formed into the figure of a person. The room suddenly became very chilly; they could see their breath. The couple abandoned their bed in panic, spending the balance of the night downstairs.

The Johnsons began asking their neighbors about the history of their house and learned that one of the previous owners, a successful screenwriter, had committed suicide in the master bedroom. A thorough investigation left no doubt of the cause of death, yet the man had been in good physical and mental health, had no financial problems, and seemed an unlikely candidate for suicide. Was the apparition in the bedroom the man's ghost or an evil spirit that drove him to kill himself?

A final confrontation occurred when Mrs. Johnson was in the haunted room, clearing out the drawers of the bureau and chest. Glancing up at the dresser mirror, she saw, to her horror, a strange man's face looming behind her. She screamed and hurriedly exited the room.

A friend advised consulting a spiritualist, who conducted a séance in the cursed room and apparently contacted the ghost. After extended negotiations with the spirit, an agreement was reached: The Johnsons would seal off that bedroom from the rest of the house, leaving the ghost in occupancy, and add a new master bedroom suite with bath to the first floor. The family would stay out of the ghost's territory, and he would confine his appearances to just the one abandoned room. It worked. Aside from occasional sounds of a person pacing the floor in the old master bedroom, life is completely peaceful and normal in the rest of the house. Sometimes it pays to reason with a ghost.

Poker Face

Some spirits are visible for minutes at a time, others for seconds. A phantom may be glimpsed for microseconds—such a brief fragment of time that the observer is not sure at all that he or she actually saw something or someone. Was that figure seen so fleetingly real or imagined? Could it have been a ghost, or was it a memory of an actual person? Some apparitions are seen for only a split second on the very edge of our vision and only as our eyes are quickly scanning, moving on before the full realization of what we've seen, or think we've seen, sinks in. The ghost of the poker player in San Francisco's St. Francis Hotel is a case in point.

Like a single frame of a motion picture, the image flashes across one's consciousness so rapidly that one can barely register it before it is gone. The balding man is so focused on the cards in his hand that he clearly is oblivious to the observer. He has a perfect poker face—a blank visage carefully neutral of any emotion. Does he hold an unbeatable hand or just random garbage? He won't tell. For some older Americans, or film buffs of any age, there is a spark of recognition, however. Could that be . . . wait a minute—if that man were smiling, wouldn't he look exactly like Al Jolson?

Al Jolson was one of the most famous American entertainers during the 1920s through 1940s. Jolson's public face was one of great animation and charm. His broad smile was legendary. He became a star in vaudeville but is most famous for his leading role in the world's first "talkie," or sound motion picture, *The Jazz Singer*, made in 1927. "Jolson sings!" boasted the ads for the movie. In the movie, Jolson played the son of an orthodox cantor who, instead of following in his father's footsteps, decided to become a jazz singer. In real life, Jolson actually was the son of a rabbi and cantor, and he made a career based on old-time minstrel shows. In an era when blacks rarely appeared before white audiences, white entertainers would appear in blackface makeup and imitate African American music styles.

Jolson really had three careers: as a minstrel singer in vaudeville, a movie star, and a grand old man of show business. Minstrel shows were declining in popularity when *The Jazz Singer* launched him into Hollywood stardom. After that memorable onscreen debut, however, Jolson appeared in a series of box-office flops, and his career faded. Then in 1946, the film *The Jolson Story* appeared, in which he dubbed all his singing but did not appear onscreen. It was a smashing success for Al, who always regarded San Francisco as his real home. He began a new career on TV and was in San Francisco to tape a guest shot on *The Bing Crosby Show* when he died at the poker table in a hotel suite, surrounded by friends. His heart attack came as he was raking in the chips, so he went out a big winner.

Maybe that's why his ghost is still playing poker at the hotel. He loved a good game among friends. Deal!

Whistling Dixie

The wispy, almost translucent figure of a beautiful woman perches atop one of many small, uniform grave markers in the vast cemetery. If it is a calm, quiet evening with little wind, she can be heard whistling the tune of "Dixie," the peppy song that became the informal anthem of the Confederacy. Anyone bold enough to approach the phantom reports that the figure fades away from view but the faint whistling persists, just barely audible to the living. Her gravestone reads "Pauline Cushman Tyler," and hers is an interesting story.

The national cemetery in San Francisco's Presidio is huge, second in size only to that in Arlington, Virginia. Pauline earned the right to be buried in a military cemetery, as she actively aided the Union cause during the Civil War and was commissioned an honorary officer in the army. She was a spy, a highly effective one, known to a few top Union commanders as the "Dixie Belle." She was a belle all right, but she used her beauty and talent against, rather than for, Old Dixie.

How the American South came to be known as Dixie probably had to do with money. In the days when banks printed their own notes, French Creole banks in New Orleans issued $10 notes marked "Dix," French for "ten." These Creole banks were solid and well managed, so the "Dixies" were accepted throughout the South at full face value, whereas the notes issued by most local banks were worth less the farther away from the issuing bank they were traded. Dixies were widely circulated by Mississippi River boatmen.

The song "Dixie" was written in 1859 by an Ohio man who performed on the fife in circuses and minstrel shows. It was an immediate hit everywhere. It was played at Jefferson Davis's inauguration as president of the Confederacy, thus becoming strongly associated with the Rebel cause, which brings us to "whistling Dixie."

Pauline Cushman Tyler was a lovely actress and singer who enjoyed entertaining the troops, both Union and Confederate. Entertainers traveled and performed anywhere—in theaters, saloons, even open fields. Pretty young women who could sing and dance were made welcome at any army camp, as Pauline discovered. She was strongly pro-Union and volunteered to spy for the North. After a tour of Confederate towns and army camps, Pauline would sneak across the battle lines and report to Union commanders.

Pauline sang "Dixie" thousands of times during her tours of the Confederate Army camps, and she sang it so enthusiastically that she became known as the "Dixie Belle." She loved the song, often humming or whistling it when alone.

Female spies served both sides during the Civil War. Most specialized in socializing with high-ranking officers, who would boast about their plans to impress the pretty girl who seemed so fascinated by them. Pauline, however, mingled more with ordinary soldiers and listened to their complaints of inadequate ammunition, lack of horses, faulty cannons, bad news from home, and ineffectual officers. They told the unvarnished truth about economic conditions and troop morale, and the Dixie Belle would dutifully report all this on her next visit back north.

In the last week of his life, Abraham Lincoln asked a band to play "Dixie" for him. The Confederacy was on the verge of its final collapse, and Lincoln declared that he'd always liked the tune, and that it had been recaptured and was again a good American song. Pauline's ghost must feel the same way, as to this day, people say they've heard her whistling "Dixie," a fine American song.

Some Revolutionary Ghosts

Revolutions are serious affairs with serious consequences—they're not supposed to be funny. The 1836 revolution in California did, however, have its moments of comic opera. The story of that uprising reads as though it were scripted by Jim Carrey and performed by the Three Stooges. The ghosts are not particularly funny, though. They seem intent on appearing dignified, as befits a governor, a general, and a whiskey distiller—all good men and true.

The three ghosts usually appear as a trio, strolling in the vicinity of the seven-acre Monterey State Historical Park. Two of the ghosts are distinguished-looking Spanish gentlemen, while the third is a rough-and-ready Yankee adventurer. These are, it is widely believed, the ghosts of Juan Bautista Alvarado, Jose Castro, and Isaac Graham, all of whom were involved in the 1836 revolution against the Mexican government. It's a long story, one that produced interesting ghosts. These ghosts, by the way, appear oblivious to the living—they ignore observers, making no effort to interact with anyone. They appear to be deep in thought and conversation with one another—as might be expected of conspirators plotting to overthrow a government.

Most Americans today would agree that California is a very special and highly desirable place, but it wasn't always so. It took a gold rush to change California's image, later reinforced by a new appreciation of its climate and further burnished by Hollywood glamour.

California once was the Spanish Empire's equivalent of Siberia—land far away on the fringes of empire and not especially important. Spain paid relatively little attention to the region. Its soldiers and administrators there sometimes went years without being paid, and nobody back in Spain cared much about what Californians were thinking or doing. After Mexico's successful overthrow of Spanish rule in 1822, little changed for California. Alta (upper) California was ruled by a governor appointed by Mexico City, more than two thousand miles from Monterey. The Mexican state of Alta California (today's California) was permitted to send one deputy to the Mexican Congress—but he didn't have a vote.

Juan Alvarado and Jose Castro decided to overthrow Governor Nicolas Gutierrez and proclaim the "Free and Sovereign State of Alta California." Gathering an army of 752 men, armed with antiquated muskets, they marched on the Monterey Presidio. They were joined by fifty Yankee adventurers led by one Isaac Graham from Tennessee. Graham had arrived in California intending to make a living as a hunter and trapper but instead set up a whiskey still and made a fortune. He didn't bother to pay taxes on his product and was happy to help overthrow a governor who did not welcome law-breaking Yankees.

This rather ragtag army demanded that Governor Gutierrez surrender. He refused. It was a standoff. Neither side was eager to spill blood. Then some of the rebels found a cannon. No one knew how to fire it. A local lawyer volunteered to read the instruction manual while others hauled the cannon close to the governor's house. After an hour with the "how to fire a cannon" booklet, the lawyer fired one shot at the governor's house. The terrified governor surrendered immediately and went back to Mexico City. Castro became acting governor, general, and commander of the Alta California Army and marching band. Alvarado became a professional politician and served as governor from 1836 to 1842. It is reported that he said he was too busy to attend his own wedding, so a friend stood in as proxy at the ceremony in the Santa Clara Mission. There is no record of what the new Mrs. Alvarado thought of this, but all husbands will agree that it probably took a lot of flowers and candy to placate her. Isaac Graham later was arrested on a charge of treason and making illegal whiskey. He was released and went right on distilling good Tennessee whiskey for thirsty Californians.

Should you spot the ghosts of the three conspirators, you might raise a glass to toast them—with Tennessee whiskey, of course.

Stay Away!

The figure of a rather stout, middle-aged woman is dressed entirely in black. The long, lace-trimmed dress represents the height of fashion a century and a half ago. She is visibly agitated, her movements abrupt and erratic, her face flushed and drenched with perspiration. The phantom's face is the picture of despair, and her dark eyes stare with a laserlike intensity. Suddenly she seems to become aware of the intruders into her overwhelming grief. "Stay away!" she warns in an agonized croak. "Typhoid! Bloody typhoid!" This is the spirit of Manuela Girardin, and you would be well advised to stay away. Not that you would catch typhoid, but Doña Manuela can be a very determined ghost.

Manuela Girardin's phantom is said to haunt the Stevenson House in the Historical Park, a seven-acre site that preserves the historical heritage of old Monterey. The building dates back to the Mexican era and was once known as the French Hotel, actually a boardinghouse. The famous English author Robert Louis Stevenson lived there for a few months in the fall of 1879, hence the name of the modest, two-story structure. Luckily for him, Stevenson had moved out before the typhoid epidemic struck in December 1879.

Typhoid is now rare, thanks to childhood inoculations against the once-dreaded disease, which is highly contagious and usually fatal. It leads to a high fever that produces a state of delirium—a time of fearsomely realistic nightmares in which the victim is raving mad.

Legend has it that Doña Manuela's husband was stricken by the dreaded disease, which was ravaging the entire community. Despite Manuela's devoted nursing, he died. Next, her two grandchildren came down with the characteristically high fever. Already exhausted from caring for her husband, she undertook the frequently futile task of nursing the little typhoid sufferers. Against the odds, they both recovered. But Doña Manuela had contracted the disease, and she was less fortunate. As her high fever raged, her brain was affected by the delirium of the final stages of the disease. Vivid nightmares plagued her. She screamed out in terror, "No, no! The devil is coming!" In her brief moments of normal thinking, she begged her family to stay away from her, fearing that they too would catch the dreaded fever and die in unimaginable agony, overwhelmed by visions of hell.

The best time—or maybe the worst time—to encounter the ghost of Doña Manuela Girardin is in December, the month of that long-ago typhoid epidemic. It is said that among the first signs of her ghostly visits is a rocking chair beginning to rock on its own. The gentle rocking gradually increases to a frantic pace, and then the rocker crashes onto its side and Manuela's screams can be heard: "Stay away! Stay away!" Maybe you really should.

Fatty's Ghost

The elegant St. Francis is one of San Francisco's grand hotels, the temporary address of the rich and famous visiting the city. Some allege that the St. Francis Hotel is inhabited by the spirits of some of its past distinguished guests. Among the ghosts said to hang out at the venerable hostelry is the rather pathetic phantom of a once-famous silent screen comedian, Fatty Arbuckle. Seldom seen these days, the ghost of Fatty Arbuckle appears to be quite depressed—

the very image of a sad clown. Fatty's tragic story is one in which fame and fortune disappeared with mind-numbing swiftness.

Suite 1221 at the St. Francis was the scene of a fatal injury to a beautiful young starlet back in 1921. It also was the scene of a fatal blow to Fatty Arbuckle's career. The obese comedian was accused of murder, a charge that, even though he was found innocent, doomed his formerly fabulous career.

The portly figure moves with surprising grace through the room. He is wearing a silk bathrobe, or lounging robe, as it was called in those days. The round, moonlike face is dominated by large, dark, expressive eyes set in pasty white flesh. The phantom's expression is one of shock and profound sorrow. Although Fatty's life did not end here at the St. Francis, his professional life surely was fatally wounded by scandal. The real tragedy may be that not only was the film star innocent of any foul play, but he may also have been the victim of a blackmail plot gone awry.

When Fatty Arbuckle drove up to San Francisco on Friday, September 3, 1921, he was looking forward to nonstop partying over the long Labor Day weekend. He and his friends had reserved a large three-bedroom suite with a private sitting room. Fatty liked to party and had a huge appetite for alcohol. Allegedly, he also enjoyed the company of young women of easy virtue. A still-credible theory is that a lovely starlet had been insinuated onto the list of party guests as part of a plot to entrap Fatty in a sex scandal, making him vulnerable to blackmail.

Fatty Arbuckle's fame and popularity as a film comedian was surpassed at the time only by that of Charlie Chaplin. He had started as one of the Keystone Kops comedy troupe and rocketed to stardom. Recently, Fatty had signed a three-year contract for the unheard-of sum of $1 million.

Fatty's supposed victim, Virginia Rappe, was found unconscious in the suite, and the rotund comedian called for an ambulance. She died in the hospital four days later from peritonitis, caused by a ruptured bladder. Rumors began to circulate that her internal injuries stemmed from intercourse with the three-hundred-pound Arbuckle. Despite the lack of evidence or eyewitnesses, Fatty was placed on trial for rape and murder. He vehemently denied having any contact with Virginia. After a sensational, circuslike trial, he was declared innocent of any wrongdoing. The jury even issued a formal apology to Fatty, who they believed should never have been brought to trial. There was reason to believe that Virginia Rappe was not a sweet, innocent girl who had been taken advantage of, but part of a setup to blackmail the wealthy star. Her fatal injury most likely had been inflicted during perverted group sex that did not involve Arbuckle.

Nevertheless, his reputation was destroyed. The few films he made after the trial were pathetic flops. Is it any wonder that Fatty Arbuckle's mournful ghost haunts the scene of the worst day of his life?

Don't Make Vampires

Don't make vampires. Sounds like good advice, doesn't it? An old story tells of how a Chinese-American family living in San Francisco a century ago learned to respect ancient traditions and not make vampires.

Although Eastern European stories of vampires, such as Dracula, are the source of most popular perceptions of the blood-drinking undead, many other cultures have tales of vampires as well. The Japanese, for example, tell stories about ghostly vampire cats, a combination that will send shivers up anyone's spine. The Navajo of America's Southwest have traditions about vampire creatures, and South Americans know that there really are vampire bats in the jungles.

Ancient Chinese tradition holds that vampires are made from deceased relatives by not honoring proper burial practices. If the dead are angry over an improper burial, they may return to haunt their families and tap their blood. Fresh blood will sustain the living dead until their bodies are respectfully reburied in correct fashion. Several generations of a San Francisco family, whom we'll call the Chans, believe that their ancestors once inadvertently created a vampire by not burying Grandpa in the proper location according to the principles of feng shui. Practitioners of feng shui are hired to advise on the orientation of structures, site selection, façade placement, and arrangement of rooms in future buildings. They also help select and orient gravesites.

Feng shui, to many Chinese, is not superstition, but an expression of proper concern that people place their structures—and their graves—in harmony with the natural order and with neighbors. Some claim, for example, that the untimely death of a movie star famous for his martial-arts films was linked to his disregard for feng shui principles in building a lavish new home in Hong Kong. And the Chans certainly learned a lesson in respect for ancient wisdom when they buried Grandpa in a grave that faced south. What followed is a horror story, but one with a happy ending.

Feng shui places great emphasis on the significance of the four cardinal directions—north, south, east and west. Old Chinese walled cities were perfectly aligned squares, with north, south, east, and west walls, each with a gate. The city always was considered to be facing south, toward the sun, the symbolic source of life. Beijing's Forbidden City, a palace complex that formed a city within a city, was designed to be approached from the south. The east gate of a city was the "spring gate," facing the sunrise. The west gate, or "autumn gate," had sacred significance, as it was believed that the spirits of deceased ancestors traveled westward to join the gods residing in the western mountains. The north gate, always in shadow, faced the bitter-cold winter winds and was the direction from which came trouble and invasion. China's Great Wall was built to keep out invaders from the north.

For the living, south is the luckiest direction and north the least lucky. But for the dead, this is reversed. According to feng shui, graves should be oriented to the north or west, never the south or east. A dead body buried facing south cannot rest and will come to life briefly in order to haunt whoever ignored feng shui until the body is reburied in proper orientation. Meanwhile, the spirit of the dead will sustain itself with fresh blood—the fresh blood of the culprit who allowed tradition to be violated.

This trouble began on the evening of Grandpa's burial. He had been a staunch traditionalist, but his family was not, and they paid no attention to the proper manner for Chinese burials. They considered themselves American, and the old customs didn't count anymore, right? Wrong. Each family member reported having the same dream the next morning. Grandpa, in an angry mood, had visited them, demanding to be reburied facing north. He bit them on the arms and sipped a little blood, then disappeared. Horrifyingly, each person had a fresh scar on the arm. They hastily called a feng shui practitioner. "Dig up the body and place it in a new grave, this time on a northward-facing slope," was his advice. The Chans did this, and the bad dreams faded away like their healing scars. Sometimes the old ways are the best ways. Rest easy, Grandpa.

Miss Mary Will Take Good Care of You

The Queen Anne is one of San Francisco's most elegant hotels. At forty-eight rooms, it is a small jewel on Sutter Street just west of Van Ness. The Queen Anne's advertised amenities include high-speed Internet, hair dryers, DVD players, and complimentary evening beverages. Its unadvertised amenities include unpacking of guest's luggage, turndown service, and being tucked in by the hotel's resident ghost, Miss Mary Lake.

The Queen Anne was built in 1890 as the Miss Mary Lake School for Girls. As many as one hundred wealthy young ladies at a time lived there, learning the social graces expected of them in those days. The school was established by a rich and influential senator, James Fall, who appointed his mistress, Mary Lake, as the school's headmistress. Miss Mary offered lessons in deportment, piano, painting and sketching, flower arrangement, household management, and the like. It can be hoped that someone other than Miss Mary taught ethics. When the senator tired of Miss Mary and replaced her with a younger mistress, the school was closed, and Miss Mary's dreams were crushed.

The building was transformed into a hotel just before the 1906 earthquake and managed to survive the quake. The frightened guests were comforted by none other than Miss Mary, who had stayed on in her beloved school-turned-hotel as a chambermaid. She was brokenhearted when her lover closed the school and spurned her. Without any money of her own, Miss Mary had little choice except to work as a maid.

Soon after Miss Mary was promoted to that great finishing school in the sky, it became evident that her spirit had not left. Apparently Miss Mary had grown into her new role in life, taking pride in looking after the hotel's guests. She had acted more like a gracious hostess than a menial servant. After her death, it seems that Miss Mary's ghost carries on her duties of making her guests comfortable.

The experience of a young couple who honeymooned at the Queen Anne is typical. After the bellboy had carried their luggage up to their room, the newlyweds decided to go downstairs for a drink. When they returned to their room, they found that someone had unpacked their bags, hung their clothing in the closet, and turned down the bedspread. A basket of fruit and candy was on a table, along with a chilled bottle of champagne. An engraved card read, "Compliments of the management." The next morning, the couple thanked the desk clerk profusely, to his evident puzzlement. "But the hotel didn't send up free champagne," he said. "Well, someone did, and we enjoyed it very much!" was the bride's reply.

A family visiting from the Midwest had a likewise pleasant encounter with Miss Mary. They had adjoining rooms so that the parents could enjoy some privacy while their six-year-old daughter slept next door. The next morning, their daughter reported that a nice maid had come into her room just as the girl was drifting off to sleep. "Night-night," she'd said as she tucked in the covers around the little girl. "Sleep well, my dear." Of course, her parents had locked and bolted the door, so it couldn't have happened. Or could it?

Other guests have reported seeing the misty form of a middle-aged woman in an old-fashioned maid's dress walking through the halls. When approached by the living, the maid simply disappears.

Enjoy your stay at the Queen Anne Hotel. Miss Mary will take good care of you.

A Hole in None

Lincoln Park lies in the highly scenic northwestern corner of San Francisco. Located within the park is what surely has to be the most beautiful municipal golf course in America. Golfers on these links face the usual hazards of sand traps, complicated by often strong winds off the ocean and frequent morning fog. There may also be some supernatural hazards, for many believe that this golf course is haunted.

Golfers just hate to lose balls. It is embarrassing to have one's skills at the game called into question, and it gets expensive too. But for novices and old pros alike, on calm or windy days, balls go missing with greater frequency at Lincoln Park than on other courses. Balls that appeared to land perfectly on the green are nowhere to be found. Balls that sailed straight down the fairway mysteriously disappear. Now, some golfers are really good at finding excuses for poor play, but the Lincoln Park Municipal Golf Course often is blamed for negative spiritual forces that are sending balls way off course, sometimes all the way to hell.

On all golf courses, small armies of treasure hunters or scavengers regularly comb the rough and sand traps or ponds for lost balls still in usable condition. Such efforts here are seldom productive. One would-be scavenger, who vows never again to visit the Lincoln Park course, even claims to have come across truly weird "ghost balls," as he calls them. These were the crumpled, empty skins of golf balls—like tiny balloons that had lost their air. The skins or outer coverings were intact, with no holes or tears, yet there was nothing inside. How could that be?

Other players, caddies, and groundskeepers swear that they've seen balls in flight slow down, change direction abruptly like the infamous "magic bullet" of the Kennedy assassination conspiracy theories, and then bury themselves forcefully in the sod. Still other observers claim they've seen balls disappear, in the air or on the ground, in a puff of smoke.

What might begin to explain all these mysteries is the fact that when pursuing their little balls across these links, golfers are walking over the bones of many dead. The Lincoln Park Municipal Golf Course is located atop what was once San Francisco's oldest and largest Chinese cemetery. In the old days, cemeteries and crematories were strictly segregated racially. San Francisco's large Chinese population had established its cemetery on the northwestern edge of the growing city. Thousands of burials had taken place there before the city, in a stunning display of callous indifference, decided to convert that land into a park. It is as though someone decided to convert a church into a bowling alley. The gravestones were removed. A "sacrifice stone," a large stone altar used for roasting whole pigs to propitiate the gods, remains as the hazard for the first tee. Some believe that a ball that has hit the sacrifice stone will never again fly true and might as well be tossed in the ocean.

So many balls appear to vanish into thin air here that they are called "holes in none." Are the spirits of the dead angry at their rest being disturbed by golfers? It does seem likely that something otherworldly is going on. Good luck with your game if you play at Lincoln Park!

The East Bay and Santa Clara Valley

THE EAST BAY IS THE PART OF THE SAN FRANCISCO METROPOLITAN region that encompasses Oakland, Berkeley, and the San Pablo and Suisun Bay communities, along with Vallejo, Concord, and Stockton. Also included in this compact region are the cities of the Santa Clara Valley, better known as Silicon Valley, as well as Hayward, San Jose, and Palo Alto. This region features a rich variety of ghosts, with a transvestite stagecoach driver, a beautiful Spanish lady waiting in vain for her Russian lover's return, the resident specter in a house built to confuse ghosts, the spirit of a peace-loving president, and the happily drunk phantoms of California's first legislators. Modern vampires and a haunted aircraft carrier add to the supernatural interest of this region.

The Vampire's Delicatessen

The believability of this story depends on how you feel about vampires. Not everyone accepts the idea that undead, supernatural beings subsist on human blood and, in the process of drinking that blood, turn their victims into vampires. The whole idea just seems too preposterous to all but a few true believers. On the other hand, vampire myths turn up in the folklore of very different cultural groups, from Eastern Europeans to the Navajo of the southwestern deserts of the United States. Is this pure coincidence, or are there deep-rooted fears common to humans that vampires once existed or even continue among us?

What if modern vampires had decided, as a matter of self-preservation, to blend in with the general population and avoid high-risk activities like attacking victims and skulking about in the middle of the night? The following is a highly controversial story based entirely on circumstantial evidence. Only one person, who wishes to remain anonymous, really believes it involves vampires.

The setting for this story is a small medical lab in Oakland that was located in a retail strip along the highway, convenient to a hospital and neighboring medical arts buildings. The medical community discovered that this lab promptly delivered accurate results. Patients were satisfied that the fees were modest and seldom required a copay.

A minor complaint, most often just a passing comment, was that some patients noted that several vials of blood, sometimes as many as six or eight, were drawn routinely. That puzzled doctors who had written scripts for only one simple test.

Whenever questioned about the seemingly excessive quantities of blood drawn for testing, the routine reply of the lab manager was that it was policy. Bureaucrats everywhere love and use that all-purpose nonanswer. "It's our policy" implies that it's customary and no reason need be supplied, take it or leave it.

One day, a lab technician who had been employed part-time to draw blood and process the paperwork was asked to work full-time and alone for several days when the manager was out with the flu. She was handed a large key ring and reminded not to enter the door marked "Private." She couldn't resist a peek. To her astonishment, the room was fitted out like an upscale cocktail lounge. Leather-padded booths lined the room, which featured a bar. Behind the bar were several large commercial refrigerators. Inside the fridges was an upsetting surprise. Vials of blood were set in racks, labeled with the age, sex, and race of the unwitting blood donor, such as "teenage female Caucasian" or "mature Asian male." She could only conclude that she had stumbled onto a blood boutique, a kind of vampires' delicatessen. Surplus vials of blood were being sold to those who were thirsty for human blood but insisted on a safe environment. Another door led directly to a secluded parking lot at the back.

Some sort of silent alarm must have alerted the proprietor, who showed up looking very agitated. "You should not have come in here," he said sternly. He reassured the obviously panicked young technician that she would not be harmed. "We have new ways; don't worry. We'll have to close the lab and relocate—a nuisance but unavoidable. We'll give you $10,000 severance pay with the hope that you won't embarrass yourself by talking about this. No one would believe you anyway."

With that, the lab was closed, and the sole witness to the vampires' delicatessen kept quiet for years, finally telling her story on the grounds of anonymity. By the way, does your neighborhood medical lab seem to draw excessive amounts of blood for testing?

Don't Sit in Dad's Chair

The Oakland family who related this story did so with the understanding that their real names not be used, so we'll call them the Andersons. This family is absolutely convinced that they are hosts to a benign but very real ghost. And the ghost is extremely possessive of a certain lounge chair, just as the living person had been. But who would believe in a haunted chair? Perhaps, on thinking about their story, you will.

The patriarch of the family was Phillip Anderson. For more than three decades, he had been a shop teacher in a middle school located in one of Oakland's southwest neighborhoods. Now, there might be tougher jobs out there—SWAT team leaders, alligator wrestlers, or bomb squad members come to mind—but not many where one is expected to corral thirty or so unruly teenagers in a room fully equipped with potentially lethal power saws, electric drills, and the like.

"I feel like a lion tamer," he used to say, "except that the lions are more predictable and have sweeter dispositions." Year after year, Phil's classes would crank out wooden coat pegs for closet doors, spice racks, wooden serving trays, and the ever-popular broom holders. In between larger projects, his students made simple doorstops by the dozen—the school had an insatiable appetite for them as they mysteriously disappeared after a few days' service.

Phil's was a frustrating and tension-ridden job. He had to be ever alert to the probability of kids maiming themselves or others, with one of the assortment of sharp edges in his shop.

In other words, Phil had really earned the right to some comfortable, peaceful rest in retirement. His legs were tired after standing all those hours—shop teachers seldom dare to sit down. On his retirement, his wife and children presented him with a luxurious lounge chair, the most expensive one in the store. It was upholstered in buttery soft leather. A lever operated a footrest. Concealed under one flip-up armrest were the controls for built-in electric heaters and a massage device. The other armrest could be raised to reveal a cup holder and storage space for books and magazines.

The chair was a big hit with Phil, who began to spend most of his waking hours in it. It was not unusual for his wife to find him sleeping all night in the chair, the result of watching late movies on TV while sipping a tall gin and tonic. Phil and the chair were practically glued together. By general agreement, no one else ever sat in Dad's chair. Other than Phil, the only other occasional occupant was Boots, the cat. Boots always vacated the chair whenever Phil came into the room, so his trespasses were accepted good-naturedly by his master.

Finally, the day came when Phil went to heaven—perhaps a special schoolteachers' heaven, where all students are quiet, interested, and not the slightest bit ornery, and school administrators are either kindly and wise or incapable of speech.

The chair remained in the place of honor—the corner with the best view of the TV. Out of habit, family members avoided sitting in it at first. But at last one adult child sat in it, tilted it back, and raised the footrest. The chair seemed to come to life abruptly. It resumed the upright position, dropped the footrest, and almost seemed to eject its occupant. No one dared to sit in it again, except Boots. The cat took brief naps in the chair, but it jumped down quickly as if sensing Phil's spirit wishing to occupy it.

Late at night, the chair's footrest would snap up of its own volition. Family members heard the soft rumble of the massager at work, and the leather seat and back became comfortably warm to the touch thanks to the heating element. Startlingly, the massager and heating features continued to function even when the chair was unplugged. Sometimes Phil's favorite mystery books would disappear from the bookshelves only to be found in the armrest pocket. It is clear to his family that Phil's spirit has chosen to revisit his little piece of paradise on earth—his chair.

Charley's Last Surprise

It would seem that California has more than its fair share of odd-balls. In fact, many residents of the other states have come to believe that California is a kind of giant magnet for eccentrics, and furthermore, that the Golden State somehow actually breeds weirdos. Whether this view of California as a giant holding tank for wackos is fair or not, it is true that the state's history has featured some truly unique characters. Take, for example, "Cockeyed Charley" Parkhurst, a famous driver for the mail stages that once ran from San Francisco to San Jose and on to Santa Cruz.

It is said that Cockeyed Charley's ghost is every bit as loud, swaggering, bold, and profane as the living stage driver. This raucous, aggressively entertaining spirit likes to show up in disreputable bars—"lowdown dives," as they were called back in the 1850s and 1860s, when Cockeyed Charley was at the height of his awesome reputation. This phantom, unmistakable by virtue of a left eye that always stares off to the extreme left regardless of where the right eye is looking, always wears dusty, stained jeans; a loudly checkered shirt topped by a red bandanna; and a black ten-gallon cowboy hat. Sometimes Charley's ghost carries a long, barbed, leather bullwhip, the emblem of the profession of stage driver. Though doubtless the whip was used often, Charley's more effective tool in keeping the horses in line and motivated was his enviable, truly awesome talent as a curser of renown. Charley was, in contemporary children's descriptive phrase, a "potty mouth."

In a profession noted for the almost continuous use of profanity, Cockeyed Charley stood out as the greatest, most creative practitioner of the art of cursing. Charley was a true artist, and his medium was obscenity, verbal mayhem, and scatological extremes. Charley would weave profane tapestries of brilliantly inventive curses, strung together in innovative combinations of offensive language. He admonished his horses to move faster and loudly commented on the mistakes and delinquent characters of other drivers.

Not too many people ever stood up to Charley. He was the toughest of a tough lot, a challenging sneer always on his clean-shaven, tobacco-juice-stained face. Gunslingers would cross to the other side of the street if they saw Charley coming.

A person of strong opinions, voiced often and loudly, Charley voted in every election and even campaigned for his favorite candidates. Charley's civic-mindedness came as a surprise to many, but his last and greatest surprise for the community came only following his death. Imagine the shock when the mortician preparing the body for burial discovered that he was a she! Papers found among Cockeyed Charley's possessions revealed that the stage driver actually was named Charlotte Parkhurst, born in New Hampshire in 1806. Charlotte evidently had decided that no one would hire a woman stage driver, so Charlotte became Charley, the very image of a hard-driving, hard-living, hard-cursing man's man.

Charlotte was buried as a man, complete with an appropriate motto on "his" tombstone: "He did it his way."

Awaiting Her Lover's Return

The misty figure of the woman, glowing with faint greenish phosphorescence, stands atop her simple tombstone, staring westward toward the Carquinez Strait. The expression on her beautiful face is one of eager anticipation, tinged with anxiety; her large, expressive eyes never blink as she scans the horizon for the ship that will bring her lover back to her at last. This spirit has been waiting a long time, since the woman's death in 1857, and the once-living woman had waited most of her life, hoping in vain to once again see her handsome, gallant lover and future husband.

The unfulfilled, rather tragic ghost is that of Doña Maria Concepcion Arguello, and she frequently appears briefly at her grave at St. Dominic's Cemetery in Benicia. Sometimes, it is said, the ghost appears in the form of a young teenage girl, dressed fashionably in aristocratic finery. Other times the phantom is a mature woman wearing a nun's habit. Maria Arguello's ghost reminds people of a romantic love that never died, a love so strong that it transcended vast distances and survived death itself.

People have long been fascinated by the theme of young love overcoming the chasm separating feuding families or different cultures, religions, or races. Doña Maria's parents, indeed her whole community, strongly disapproved of her choice of a future husband. Maria was Spanish and her fiancé was Russian, which made them official enemies, or at least uneasy rivals, in colonial California.

Spanish colonial control over California was a bit uncertain in the early 1800s. A handful of administrators, soldiers, and priests were charged with holding the land for Spain, but being on the fringe of its empire, California was a low priority for the Spaniards. When Russian explorers and adventurers, based in Alaska, boldly sailed along Northern California's coast, the small numbers of poorly equipped Spanish soldiers could do little to stop them. War was not declared, but the Spaniards clearly were uneasy about Russian ambitions.

Doña Maria's father, Don Luis Arguello, was commandant of the San Francisco presidio, Spain's northernmost military post. In April 1806, a Russian ship entered the harbor with an important passenger aboard. Count Nikolai Petrovich Rezanov, a high-ranking diplomat and soldier, wanted to purchase grain, potatoes, and fresh vegetables for the Russians' outpost in Sitka, Alaska, as the region couldn't grow the food they needed. The tall, blue-eyed, handsome Russian count made a big impression on the commandant's sixteen-year-old daughter. Maria was instantly attracted to Count Rezanov, who returned her intense interest. By the time the Spanish finally, though reluctantly, agreed to sell supplies to the Russians, the count had proposed to Maria over the strong objections of her father. Rezanov explained that as a distant cousin of the tsar, he needed the ruler's permission to marry a non-Russian. He would have to travel all the way back to St. Petersburg, halfway around the world, to plead his case with the tsar. Would Maria wait for his return? "Forever!" she promised, yearning for the day they could wed.

That day never came. Unbeknownst to Maria, the count died during his long, difficult journey across the frozen wastes of Siberia. Brokenhearted when her lover never came back, Maria eventually became a Dominican nun and taught at St. Catherine's Seminary until her death in 1857. Her spirit, still faithful to her handsome Russian, peers eagerly toward the sea, awaiting her betrothed.

Listen to Your Mother-in-Law

Somehow one just doesn't associate a modern tract house with hauntings or evil spirits. It is perfectly believable that ancient castles would have a ghost or two in residence, but ancient castles are nonexistent in places like Berkeley. Gloomy, old Victorian mansions are almost expected to feature ghosts, and there is no shortage of those in California cities, but this particular haunted house—or maybe it was a possessed house—was supremely ordinary. It was a typical California ranch home, only about ten years old at the time. The house looked almost exactly like its neighbors, with the standard two-car garage at the front and a small in-ground pool in the backyard. So ordinary, yet so uniquely disturbing in what followed when a young family moved in.

We'll call them the Greens—Mom, Dad, and little Taylor, then about four years old. At last they had been able to move out of an apartment into their own home. One of the charms of the house, in the view of the husband, was that it was a good hour and a half from his mother-in-law's place. He had never gotten along well with her. She took every opportunity to intrude in the lives of her daughter's family. With strong opinions on all subjects, she unhesitatingly gave advice about everything. She considered herself a very religious woman and constantly reminded everyone of her daily attendance at mass. Her daughter and son-in-law were, in her opinion, living like heathens, as they seldom went near a church. The old lady was particularly outraged that her grandson had not been christened. Her complaints about that led to the Greens calling her "Our Lady of Criticism" behind her back. Way behind her back, as she did not take criticism with any grace.

When it became apparent that the Greens' new house contained some sort of evil spirit, Our Lady of Criticism really earned her title. The trouble began the first night little Taylor spent in his bedroom. The window began rattling as though a tornado was approaching, yet it was a calm evening. The room, already noticeably cooler than the rest of the house, became freezing in temperature. Soon after drifting off to sleep, Taylor woke up screaming, as though from a bad dream. The little boy insisted on a nightlight, but it would not stay lit. Its new replacement similarly malfunctioned. One morning, a heavy chest of drawers lay facedown on the floor. Other mornings found furniture rearranged by some force far beyond Taylor's muscle capacity. Taylor wasn't sleeping well at all and frequently woke his parents with unearthly screaming. He variously described lions, bears, or wolves coming into his room and menacing him in his bed. His parents heard odd creaking noises and footsteps in his room when Taylor was lying still in bed.

Taylor's grandmother was, as usual, full of advice—good advice, as it turned out. "Get Taylor baptized," she demanded, "and ask a priest what to do." Taylor was duly baptized. Asked to perform an exorcism, the priest pointed out that although the church did have such a rite, it was rarely used. Instead, he volunteered to visit the house and bless Taylor's room with a sprinkling of holy water. At his grandmother's insistence, a large metal crucifix was hung above Taylor's bed, and a small medal depicting the Madonna and child was pinned to his one-piece sleepers.

What followed was the first truly peaceful night the Greens had spent in that house. Oddly, the next morning revealed that the wall behind the crucifix looked slightly scorched, as though the metal had been red hot. Had some sort of supernatural struggle taken place between the forces of good and evil? The Greens will never know, but they have become regular churchgoers. Even mothers-in-law can be right sometimes.

No, No More!

The house sits on a quiet side street convenient to the California State University at Hayward. The structure has seen better days. The siding is shabby, and the exterior paint was fresh back when Ronald Reagan was governor. Even the weeds in the yard look dejected. The house has sunk to the bottom of the residential market food chain—it is rented to college students, a group not noted for their tender loving care of rental properties. The owners of this particular house, however, actually prefer students as tenants. Because a fresh crop of students arrive every summer looking for housing, many of them have never heard about the house's evil reputation. The haunted house's tenants have often left before the end of the fall semester, even though their lease runs until June.

Residents usually discover the presence of their supernatural roommate within a month or so of moving in. Commonly, nothing unusual happens during the first weeks. It is almost as though the ghost is quietly observing the new arrivals before making its presence known. The experience of a recent group is typical. The first alert to paranormal activity was the behavior of the cat. Although pets were prohibited by the lease, one softhearted female student decided to take in a stray that would hang about the house, hopeful that young adults far from home might take pity on it. The cat's friendliness and willingness to eat leftover pizza sealed the deal. The cat was dubbed Tiger in ironic tribute to its amiable good nature. Tiger would cuddle on anyone's lap and make itself at home everywhere but the upstairs back bedroom. The cat adamantly refused to enter the room. Once, when carried in someone's arms, he laid his ears back, bristled his fur, and made uncharacteristic use of his claws in beating a panicky exit.

It took weeks before Tiger's human family finally understood the cat's avoidance of the room. One of the girls sleeping in the back bedroom was beginning to hear faint crying late at night, as though a TV had been left on. On successive nights, the crying gradually grew louder and more intensive. Finally the misty, phosphorescent image of a little girl appeared and wailed, "No! No more, please no more!" Then abruptly, the figure disappeared. This unnerving event was repeated every night until the room's inhabitants moved their beds into the onetime dining room downstairs.

One of the other tenants, a history major, decided to do a little research on the house's past. A neighbor had mentioned that he thought a murder might have been committed there back in the mid-1970s. Sure enough, a search of microfiches of back issues of the local newspaper revealed a horrifying story. An eight-year-old girl had been found strangled to death in an upstairs bedroom. The autopsy had shown that she had been sexually molested, repeatedly and brutally. Her widowed stepfather eventually was convicted of her murder and only recently had died in prison.

Apparently the severely traumatized spirit of the little girl had never left the scene of her torment and death. "No! No more," she still pleads. "No more!" One can only pray that somehow, someday, she will find peace and leave the house.

The Merry Spirits

Most people probably would just as soon not meet any ghosts. It can be an unsettling, even horrifying experience. Some ghosts, after all, seem to deliberately try to frighten the living and even may attempt to harm anyone they encounter. On the other hand, some ghosts ignore the living and seem totally absorbed in their own spiritual world. Such ghosts often appear to be having such a grand time that they are oblivious to any living observers. Maybe being quite drunk makes these carousing ghosts harmless and, indeed, rather funny. Let's face it: If you are going to meet some ghosts, it would be better if those phantoms were happily inebriated and not the slightest bit interested in harassing the living. The merry spirits of California's very first legislature fill the bill.

Although the state constitution was drafted and signed in Monterey's Colton Hall, the first legislature convened in San Jose, making that city California's first state capital. San Jose served as the capital for only two years, 1849 to 1851, when the capital was moved first to Benicia, and then finally, in 1854, to Sacramento. Given the raucous and unseemly behavior of the state's first legislators, San Jose's citizens probably were happy to see them depart. All except the saloonkeepers, of course.

The merry spirits of the first legislators have been seen to appear, some claim, in City Hall Park, the open area that is closest to the site of the first capital in downtown San Jose. The first legislative session opened on December 15, 1849, and December remains the most likely time to see the merry spirits cavort. That first gathering of state lawmakers became known as the "legislature of a thousand drinks"; this is your first clue to the goings-on. As a contemporary report noted, "The legislators were good drinkers—they drank like men. If they could not stand the ceremony on any particular occasion, they would lie down to it with a becoming grace."

Starting what seems to have become a tradition, the lawmakers also recruited a large complement of what were referred to as "ladies of easy virtue"—women whose affections were negotiable. These ladies came from all corners of California to help soothe away the cares of legislators weary from a strenuous day of arguing about new laws.

Today, it is said, the shades of legislators and their ladies of convenience dance a drunken fandango in the late-night hours in San Jose. They whirl about in the frenetic dance before reeling off in search of another alcohol-induced stupor, oblivious of each other as well as of any living witnesses.

Never mind the ultimately distressing, if somewhat humorous, drunkenness of the merry spirits of long-dead legislators. It's not as if they were doing anything important—just creating the rules by which law-abiding citizens live and work.

The Phantom Protester

San Jose is an interesting combination of old and new. It is California's first town, as distinguished from missions and presidios, having been established in 1777. It served briefly as the state's first capital, from 1849 to 1851. San Jose's chief claim to fame was once that it packed and shipped a third of the world's prunes. Now it has become the capital of world-famous Silicon Valley, a center for computer hardware and software.

The town is also home to San Jose State University, whose roots go back to 1862, making it the oldest public educational institution in California. As happens at most great universities, San Jose State frequently generates and hosts public demonstrations, marches, protests, or rallies advocating social and political causes. It is at such events that the phantom marcher shows up. This unique ghost has become a kind of patron saint of protest. There is no way to be sure whose ghost it may be, but many believe it is the shade of the poet Edwin Markham. The phantom's behavior and the poet's history both support this identification.

Edwin Markham was born in 1852. He attended San Jose State Normal School, the predecessor of the university, and went on to a career as a schoolteacher and administrator. In 1898, in a house in San Jose now owned by the university, Markham wrote "The Man with the Hoe," which earned him international recognition as a poet. He became a well-known socialist and mystic, often participating in rallies and marches.

The mysterious figure is that of an elderly man dressed in flannel trousers and a tweed jacket with leather patches at the elbows, classic campus fashion in the 1930s. Looking very much like a scholarly professor, the slightly stooped figure marches along with the group, sometimes carrying a handmade sign, or stands at the back of a protest gathering, nodding in agreement with the speakers. This apparition has the air of a gentlemanly rebel, which is exactly what the living man personified.

The phantom protester can be counted on to show up to support virtually any and all left-wing causes. In the 1950s, the ghost appeared to help protest nuclear testing. The 1960s causes of civil rights advancement and Vietnam protests were graced by the supernatural supporter. All the way to the present, any cause popular enough to draw a crowd on campus brings out the phantom protester.

The ghost shows support by its presence only. It does not interact with the living. If anyone attempts to draw it into a conversation, thinking they're talking to a living soul, the ghost just nods politely and walks away, soon disappearing. An expression of carefully considered support and agreement seems permanently fixed on the handsome face, although one fellow protester noted a puzzled expression at a "save the whales" rally. Perhaps the spirit, being out of touch for fifty years, didn't quite understand why whales needed saving. Since Markham's death in 1940, his ghost apparently continues to have enthusiasm for left-wing causes. The phantom protester marches on.

The Peaceable Spirit

Just looking at the expression on this phantom's face is enough to tell you whether the nation is at peace or at war. The questions of war or peace always were of prime importance to the living man and continue to be a concern to his spirit. Ironically, the man's place in history has emphasized his perceived failures and not his considerable achievements. He'd hoped to be remembered as a man who consistently worked for peace, charity, and efficiency in government. Instead, his public image became that of an inept blunderer who couldn't seem to comprehend, much less cope with, an economic crisis. Meet the ghost of Herbert Clark Hoover, thirty-first president of the United States.

President Hoover's phantom takes the form of a rather rotund, balding, late middle-aged man. He is wearing a very conservative three-piece, dark blue pinstriped suit, and his round, fleshy face seldom bears a smile. His expression is either that of bland distraction, deep in thought, or, more likely these days, deeply frowning at bad news. War, or the threat of war, is bad news indeed to Hoover, whose life was shaped by his concerns to aid the victims of war and try to prevent it.

His spirit is said to frequent the Hoover Tower, a prominent landmark on the campus of Stanford University in Palo Alto. The 285-foot-tall tower houses the Hoover Institution on War, Revolution and Peace, a public-policy research center devoted to the study of world conflict. Herbert Hoover founded and endowed the institution in 1919, shortly after the end of World War I and some nine years before his election as president.

Orphaned at age nine, Hoover was big on self-reliance. His interest in fostering peace traces back to the influence of his mother, an ordained Quaker minister. He earned a degree in geology and mining engineering at Stanford. His work in developing mines took him to China, where he observed firsthand the poverty prevailing in underdeveloped countries. Hoover became a millionaire through his expertise and skillful money management. He had a reputation for being a superbly efficient manager, and President Woodrow Wilson asked him to organize American relief efforts in Europe. Hoover headed the Committee for Belgian Relief, the U.S. Food Administration for Europe, and the American Relief Administration.

His efforts at organizing food shipments probably saved millions of lives, and he became so popular that both political parties urged him to run for president in 1920. Hoover declined on the grounds that he needed experience in government, serving instead as secretary of commerce under Presidents Warren Harding and Calvin Coolidge. Hoover's presidency, from 1929 to 1933, is forever associated with the onset of the Great Depression. He was blamed, fairly or unfairly, for this economic and social disaster. Hoover supported American policy in World War II but became a vocal critic of the Cold War policy based on nuclear weapons. He returned to his longtime interest in preventing war, and it seems that his spirit maintains his deep conviction that wars must be avoided if at all possible.

Rough Justice, Gruesome Ghosts

Is there a more horrific crime than kidnapping? Maybe, but surely kidnapping is on everyone's top-ten list. Kidnapping imposes severe psychological torture on the victims and their families—stress that may last for days, weeks, even months before resolution. And the period of uncertainty regarding a victim's fate too often is terminated by the discovery of a dead body.

A brutal kidnapping ending in cold-blooded murder led to a famous lynching, which apparently led in turn to the production of two particularly gruesome ghosts. These ghosts haunt a lovely little urban park—St. James Park in downtown San Jose. In broad day-light, the park is a place of peaceful pleasure, filled with flowers and shrubs set among towering palms and oaks. But at night and into the early hours of dawn, the misty, slightly fluorescent forms of two men can be seen hanging from tall trees, their bodies slowly twisting as though in a strong breeze. Those unfortunate enough to see these apparitions up close still shut their eyes at the memory of the faces contorted with fear and pain, eyes bulging and tongues protruding grotesquely as the hanged men slowly strangle to death.

These tormented ghosts are believed to be the spirits of two pro-foundly evil men who kidnapped the young son of a wealthy local merchant and then murdered him, probably following a lengthy period of torture and obscene abuse. They were brought to rough justice at the hands of an enraged mob, and the true justice of their lynching was so obvious that the governor of California publicly approved the mob action of delivering swift punishment for their crimes. It became a local tradition, or superstition, that the names of these two notorious criminals not be spoken or printed, lest this noto-riety enable their ghosts to escape their nooses and wander the streets in search of more innocent victims of their cruel and violent actions.

The year was 1933, in the depths of the Great Depression, and the particularly cruel and inhumane crime of kidnapping was on everyone's mind. Early the previous year, the most publicized kid-napping in American history had occurred: the abduction and mur-der of the twenty-month-old son of America's hero, pioneering aviator Charles Lindbergh. Within months of this notorious kidnap-ping, Congress passed a law dubbed the Lindbergh Act, which brought the FBI into the investigation of the crime if the kidnappers crossed state boundaries or used the U.S. mail to deliver ransom demands. The Lindbergh Act did not, as was popularly believed, impose the death penalty on convicted kidnappers; it said nothing about appropriate punishment. Public opinion was, however, clearly in favor of the death penalty for such horrific cruelty.

The San Jose kidnapper-murderers were caught soon after their little victim's body was discovered. A rumor spread that the boy had been tortured and sexually abused before being killed. The coroner's office did not deny this rumor. A defense attorney, in an interview in a local paper, unwisely gave the opinion that the two culprits might escape the death penalty on the grounds of insanity. That did it. A howling mob descended on the city jail and dragged the accused to the nearby park, where they were unceremoniously and inexpertly hanged. Whereas a professional hangman and scaffold would have produced a quick death by snapping the spinal column, the amateurish hanging resulted in slow, agonizing strangulation, which did not dismay the angry crowd.

Today some still claim to have seen the phantoms of the two hanged kidnappers twist slowly at the ends of their ropes. Stay clear of St. James Park in the late-night and early-morning hours, and don't speak the names of the damned.

House of Mystery, House of Ghosts

Pity poor Sarah Winchester. For most of her adult life, she lived in a state of unrelieved abject terror. It could be said that she was deathly afraid of death itself, and that unreasoning fear drove her to devote her life to postponing her death. Sarah Winchester died in 1922, but many believe that her spirit, still terrified by the thought of death, has not been able to move on to the next plane of existence, that world of eternal light and love that many of us believe awaits us on the other side.

Sarah Winchester's ghost is said to haunt the vast mansion she built in San Jose, a house that has become a major tourist attraction. The Winchester Mystery House at 525 South Winchester Boulevard is unique in that it was designed to frustrate the evil spirits who Sarah believed wished to harass her and caused her death.

Although she was fabulously wealthy as the heiress to the Winchester arms fortune, life had not been kind to Sarah. Her beloved husband had died at an early age, and their two children followed him to the grave shortly thereafter. Overwhelmed by grief, Sarah began holding séances, attempting to communicate with her deceased loved ones. The spirits of her husband and children apparently could offer no solace or calm her dread of death. Inevitably, she consulted a spiritualist as to when she would die. It took several agonizing sessions before Sarah was told that she would die on the very day that her new house, then under construction, was completed. For Sarah Winchester, backed by a huge fortune, the answer was simple: Don't stop building the house.

The architect's plans for the Winchester Mansion called for a seventeen-room structure, plenty of space for a widow who seldom went out and never entertained. The house, begun in 1884, could never be declared finished, in her view. She hired as many as sixteen carpenters at a time and kept them busy with additions and constant remodeling. Sarah held séances every evening and was convinced that evil spirits were attempting to crash her supernatural parties. The Winchester Mansion grew to 160 rooms, so many that the daily séances could be held in a different room for more than five months without repeating a location.

Evidently Sara thought that evil spirits could be prevented from haunting her by creating an impenetrable and confusing maze of a house. Ancient beliefs hold that Satan and his minions can travel only in straight lines and cannot cross running water. Sarah apparently decided that Satan also couldn't cope with doors that opened onto blank walls, stairs that led nowhere, outer doors that opened to sheer drops of twenty feet, and secret passageways. Her house ended up with two thousand doors, ten thousand windows, forty-seven fireplaces, and forty staircases. Sarah and her servants even had to carry maps to find their way through the maze of rooms.

The widow Winchester also was convinced that her family was haunted and cursed by the spirits of the thousands of people who had met death by the agency of Winchester guns. She was fearful that these ghosts were intent on vengeance on her family. It's likely she would have disagreed with the National Rifle Association's assertion that "guns don't kill people; people kill people."

When death finally came for Sarah in 1922, she had spent $5.5 million on building and remodeling her house. The hammering and sawing sounds were stilled at last. Sarah's ghost is said to still wander about the labyrinthine house, her terror undiminished as she desperately tries to evade the malignant spirits that plagued her in both life and death.

The Tree of Knowledge

What is the nature of the relationship between people and the environment—living and nonliving—around them? This is a question as old as the Garden of Eden and as contemporary as national political campaigns. Does the physical world, including all forms of life, both plant and animal, exist only to be used by humans, or is there a more complex and moral relationship between humans, said to be the "crowning glory of creation," and the rest of creation?

The Bible teaches that humans have been given domain over the earth, over all the creatures that fly in the sky, walk or crawl on land, or swim in the sea. Dominion signifies more than domination, however. It means responsibility, not just exploitation; it is supposed to be a two-way relationship, and a moral one.

The pre-Christian native Californians, who believed that the Great Spirit was manifested in all the splendors of creation, certainly would have agreed. They especially were spiritually impressed by the redwood trees, which commonly grow more than two hundred feet high. These trees always seem to impress everyone who sees them, and comparisons of groves of the majestic trees to cathedrals are common.

When California's first Spanish governor, the great explorer Gaspar de Portola, was marching toward his discovery of San Francisco Bay, he witnessed an impressive sight. The local Indians at what is now Palo Alto were described as "very affable, mild and docile and very generous." In fact, they may well have been nicer than the invading Spanish. They believed that a divine spirit dwelled in a particular redwood tree, and they held their councils beneath it. This towering tree was unusual in that it had two massive trunks that were joined at the base, making a huge V. The Indians believed that this unique feature served to channel spiritual communications: One trunk could transmit messages from the people to the Great Spirit, and the other was the conduit for guidance from the Great Spirit down to his people.

The councils held beneath this great tree were renowned for their wise and farsighted consensus. The Spaniards took to holding deliberations at the double tree as well. The double-trunked redwood became such a symbol of wisdom and revealed knowledge that it appears to this day on the seal of Stanford University, whose campus was created when the tree still lived.

Do the giant redwoods contain any mystical power of communicating knowledge of divine wisdom? Can they somehow channel spiritual advice to those who respectfully contemplate the beauty of creation beneath the redwoods, seeking a true understanding of nature? Try it—there are plenty of redwoods in Northern California.

The Haunted Aircraft Carrier

The massive bulk of the aircraft carrier looms high above its dock. All is quiet on the great ship as the sun rises in the east over the city of Oakland. To the west are the still, dark waters of San Francisco Bay, with the twinkling lights of the Bay Bridge glowing through the early-morning fog. A lone marine paces along the enormous flight deck, rifle over his shoulder as he patrols. There is nothing unusual about the scene except for one thing: The marine guard is a ghost.

The USS *Hornet* is a ship of ghosts—the ghosts of those who served aboard her, and some who died aboard her, in her long and illustrious service to America. The *Hornet* was launched in 1943, at the height of World War II. She was a giant of her day, the first U.S. Navy vessel built too large to fit through the Panama Canal, although she seems modest in size now compared to today's nuclear-powered carriers. The *Hornet* saw action in World War II and Vietnam. Near the end of her active service, she was the main recovery vessel retrieving lunar capsules as they splashed down in the Pacific. The *Hornet*'s long history evidently has produced many ghosts.

No one is quite sure exactly who the ghosts are or what their motivation might be for remaining aboard. It is known that over the years, men did die on the *Hornet*—sailors and marines hit by enemy fire, naval airmen who, though seriously wounded in the air, managed to bring their crippled aircraft back to the carrier, even one or two personnel stricken by heart attacks during the stress of battle. It has been theorized that some spirits of those killed in battle are too traumatized to move on to the spirit realm, while other spirits remain at their posts out of a strong sense of duty and loyalty.

The young officer in dress blues, brass shining and shoes newly polished, gives a smart salute to the tourist couple coming up the gangway. The wife, charmed, takes a moment to get out her camera and snap his picture. When the film is developed, it shows a picture of the *Hornet* in bright sunshine. The focus is sharp, but there is no welcoming officer.

A bandage-swathed, bloody figure, presumably a dummy, lies on a cot in the sick bay, part of the guided tour. When a visitor turns to take another look, the figure has vanished.

Many of those who visit the USS *Hornet*, now permanently berthed at Alameda Point in the former U.S. Naval Air Station at

Alameda, feel that they are sharing the venerable vessel with ghosts. Enjoy your tour. The *Hornet* is well worth a visit, even if you don't meet a ghost or two.

In the Stillness

Over time, Ken Smith grew to dread the time he called the "stillness." The stillness was the very early morning, the hours between 2 and 4 A.M., when most of the people in Hayward were sound asleep. But the ghosts were awake—and agitated and noisy.

It took a long time for Ken to admit to himself that a) there were such things as ghosts; b) somehow his house was infested with them; and c) he was really scared. Not that he would ever confess any of this to another living soul—he couldn't; it would destroy his image as a cool, rational, diligent scholar. Ken was a professor of history at California State University at Hayward. In the academic community, image is everything, even more so than in other career fields.

The ghosts didn't bring themselves to Ken's attention until he'd been in the house for a few months. After his wife had died, long after their chicks had left the nest for successful careers of their own, Ken decided to downsize and sell his four-bedroom house. He chose a charming, compact cottage within easy walking distance of the university. The real estate lady had called it a "classic craftsman," a two-bedroom charmer that was perfect for him. Perfect, that is, until the mysterious voices started up.

Actually, it was Winston who first sensed the spirits' presence. Winston was an English bulldog, named for his courage, after Winston Churchill, one of Ken's favorite historic figures. Winston looked like a dog you wouldn't want to mess with, what with his slightly bowlegged, aggressive stance and bold stare, but actually, he was a real softy. He was quietly affectionate with Ken and a real deterrent to would-be burglars, door-to-door salesmen, and pesky religious missionaries. Winston had never shown fear—not until that day in the basement.

Ken had accumulated hundreds of books over the years. He decided to construct bookshelves along a wall in the basement, where an outside wall offered a suitable area for built-ins. Very dated 1960s-style Philippine mahogany paneling covered the wall—

it would have to go. As Ken soon discovered, however, the paneling was a false wall, hiding a narrow space behind it that ran the width of the basement. Ken's deconstruction revealed a clever hidden door in the false wall, giving access to the unsuspected space. In the secret room were puzzling relics of some bizarre use or occupancy. A toilet and sink had been installed, and an air vent supplied heat or air-conditioning. A narrow iron cot occupied a corner, and a heavy steel table was bolted to the outer wall. Ominously, several heavy steel rings were anchored in the concrete walls. It looked like a jail cell.

Winston cautiously entered the secret room, sniffing apprehensively. Suddenly the dog turned tail, howling as though in pain, and ran up the stairs as if pursued by demons. He would never again venture into the basement.

Ken used his research skills to look into the history of the house. It had been previously owned by a professor of mathematics at Cal State. Ken hadn't known him; mathematicians and historians, working in different buildings on the sprawling 325-acre campus and sharing no interests, could teach there for thirty years and barely recognize one another.

The numbers guy, as Ken thought of him, had been a reclusive bachelor with no known relatives and, apparently, few friends. Why had he built a hidden cell in his basement? When Ken inquired of his neighbors, a chilling picture of the previous owner emerged. He was universally described as being very quiet, limiting socialization to brief greetings. "A nice enough guy, but we barely got to know him," was the consensus. It occurred to Ken that people usually described serial killers in the same terms.

A horrible suspicion began to form in Ken's mind. The secret room looked like a jail cell because that was just what it had been. A search of Hayward's local newspaper archives revealed a frightening pattern. Over the years, a series of mysterious disappearances had occurred. Young female university students had gone missing after spring break or during summer vacation. They didn't return to school, even to retrieve personal possessions from dorm rooms. They hadn't gone home either. They'd simply vanished, as do thousands of people every year across the country. Had they done time in the mathematician's secret cell before disappearing from the world of the living?

Ken began having very disturbing dreams—or were they just dreams? He would hear faint cries and moans during the early-morning stillness. The voices, which seemed to come from the basement, pleaded for meals and promised cooperation and submission. Sometimes he heard agonizing screams and moans as though someone were being tortured.

Nothing would provide sound, uninterrupted sleep—not sleeping pills, not four or five gin and tonics, not even a puff or two on homemade smokes. The stillness brought nightly terror.

Ken put the house on the market at an attractively low price. It sold quickly, and he moved to the other side of town. He has since heard that it is for sale again. Looking for a bargain? Do you sleep soundly through the early-morning stillness? Good luck.

Witness to the Future

How's this for a scary dream? There's a terrible rumbling sound, as though an impossibly huge freight train is passing close by in the midst of a brutal thunderstorm. Shortly afterward, the loud screams of hundreds of people reach a panicked crescendo, which then trails off to solitary wails. The ground itself appears to move as though it has become more liquid than solid; a wavelike ripple appears to move over the surface. In the city, showers of bricks, building stones, and other debris rain down from the upper floors of trembling tall buildings. Multiple fires break out simultaneously as gas mains rupture under the streets. More than five hundred people lose their lives, and thirty thousand buildings are destroyed. Four square miles, once the heart of a great city, are leveled by the force of the earthquake or the fearsome firestorm that followed.

All of this happened when the great San Francisco earthquake hit at 5:16 A.M. on April 18, 1906. That is history, and it is also history that the disaster was predicted by the man known as the "Holy Man of Santa Clara," one Fray Maguin de Catala, who served Mission Santa Clara de Asis two centuries ago. He foresaw, he said, a mighty earthquake destroying San Francisco. He did not report all the details, not did he have any sense of the timing of the disaster, but he did see it during a dream, or perhaps a trance. His vision of catastrophe came to him several times, more than a century before the great earthquake of 1906.

Fray Maguin de Catala certainly would have been aware of earthquakes. His own mission, founded in 1777, was severely damaged in the quakes of 1812 and 1818. But earthquakes were not the only notable event that he prophesied. According to local legend, Catala also foresaw the conquest of California by the United States. He predicted that vast quantities of gold would be discovered, attracting new waves of adventurers to the area.

Was the Holy Man of Santa Clara somehow blessed with the ability to see into the future? Had he earned the gift of prophesy by his life of devotion and good works? Or was the ability to peer into the future more of a curse than a gift?

Mission Santa Clara is the only old mission located on a university campus. The present structure, built in 1927, is the fifth church on this site (this really is earthquake country). It contains the original memorial to Fray Maguin de Catala, where several visitors have had unexplained, rather frightening experiences while at prayer.

One student claims to have foreseen the destruction of the World Trade Center towers in New York on September 11. A faculty member at the university, who wishes to remain anonymous, reports having strange visions while praying near the holy man's memorial. He saw another great San Francisco earthquake. In his trance-like dream, which may have lasted for only a few seconds, he saw the beautiful Transamerica Pyramid Tower sway. It did not collapse, but a deadly hail of broken window glass injured many in the streets below. In the vision, the great towers of the Golden Gate Bridge trembled but did not fall. The roadway, however, buckled and collapsed.

The most disturbing images of the future disaster were of floods. Apparently this next major quake will destroy the dams that created Upper and Lower Crystal Springs Reservoirs, along with San Andreas Lake. Just when San Francisco will desperately need water to fight the fires that follow major quakes, the reservoirs will be empty.

Does the spirit of Fray Maguin de Catala somehow communicate his own visions of the future to people praying near his memorial? A small but growing number of believers think so. Would you like to see the future? You could try praying earnestly at Fray Catala's memorial. But be warned—the future you might glimpse could be scary.

The Sacramento Valley

THIS LARGE REGION FOCUSES ON CALIFORNIA'S GREAT CENTRAL VALLEY from Merced to Redding and between the Sierra on the east and the Coast Ranges to the west. Sacramento, the state capital, is California's fourth-largest metropolitan area. Gold was first discovered in this region, but its present wealth is based more on the agricultural productivity of the valley. The Sacramento Valley features an interesting variety of ghosts, including the victims of a steamboat disaster, a bloody stagecoach holdup, and an infamous massacre of American Indians. Among the valley's tales of the supernatural are those of a family picnic that was visited by a UFO, a grandmother reincarnated as a cat, the ghost of modern California's godfather, a cat that could foretell the future, and a preacher who outran the Devil.

Grandma Has Claws

Is reincarnation real? Can the spirit or soul of the deceased return to this plane of existence in another body? Although hundreds of millions of people in other parts of the world firmly believe in it, relatively few Americans accept the idea of physical reincarnation. A family in Chico, however, is absolutely convinced that not only can it happen, it has happened. They know that Grandma has come back.

The family, whom we'll call the Jacksons, had been living with their reincarnated grandmother for several years. They are convinced that she has come back as a cat, which some family members think is entirely appropriate, given Grandma's personality.

It was only a few months after Grandma had, presumably, gone to heaven. She had lived in her own house until her last breath, cared for by a devoted granddaughter and her family. Grandma had gotten a little cranky in her old age but basically was a generous and warmhearted person. She did like things her way, however, and could be very particular about her food and comforts. She was sadly missed, but not for long.

The cat showed up one bright morning on the Jacksons' porch. She was mewing loudly, and when the granddaughter went to see what was happening, the cat quickly took advantage of the partly opened door. Uninvited, the cat edged past the granddaughter and promptly settled into a large, velvet wingback chair that had been Grandma's favorite. This cat seemed to act as though she owned the chair, the entire house, and the family. Intriguingly, the cat wore a beautiful rhinestone-studded collar bearing an engraved nameplate that read, "Cuddles." Now, Cuddles had been Grandpa's affectionate nickname for Grandma. No doubt Grandma was her husband's Cuddles—they had seven children—but she didn't seem like a Cuddles to the rest of her family. No one else but Grandpa even dared call her Cuddles to her face, but it became an ironic nickname behind her back.

Cuddles the cat was a beautiful Siamese with creamy fur blending to a rich chocolate on her face, paws, and tail. Her gorgeous blue eyes were slightly crossed. Assuming that Cuddles was absent without leave from a frantic owner, the Jacksons advertised in the local paper to locate her owner. There was no response. The veterinarian who examined Cuddles assured the Jacksons that she was quite healthy and about a year old. "She must have some Burmese in her," he joked. Burmese cats are famous for being very vocal, which Cuddles certainly was. The cat seemed to be constantly meowing. As cats will, Cuddles set about training her human family in the care and comfort of cats. When offered cheap dried cat food, she went hungry for a day, finally gulped down a few mouthfuls, then regurgitated back into her bowl. The Jacksons learned their lesson and began buying gourmet canned cat food. Although she usually ignored the television, the Jacksons swear that Cuddles fixated on the screen during reruns of *The Golden Girls*, Grandma's favorite.

Grandma's favorite chair became Cuddles's chair. Anyone bold enough to sit in it risked a confrontation with the feline's claws. Removing her from the chair provoked anguished meowing and bared fangs. Cuddles responded to people exactly as Grandma had: The cat treated affectionately those whom Grandma had favored but ignored those not beloved by the old lady.

Is Cuddles really the reincarnation of Grandma? The Jacksons think so, and it seems as if Cuddles does too.

Picnicking with a UFO

On a lovely day in spring, a Redding family whom we'll call the Scotts decided to have a picnic lunch at nearby Whiskeytown National Recreation Area. A favorite place for relaxing was along the lakeshore, so that's where they headed. What started as a fun family afternoon, though, turned out to be a truly unforgettable experience when a UFO showed up as an uninvited guest.

The Scotts hiked in to a rather secluded part of the lakeshore, far from the dam. No sooner had they set up their picnic stuff when they noticed a fast-moving shadow pass overhead. Looking up, they saw a round, bulbous craft that closely resembled a child's top as it spun rapidly on its axis. It appeared to be a dull silver in color, with bluish green lights blinking rapidly on and off in sequence around its rim. There was a low, barely audible hum from the craft, much like that experienced when passing under high-tension electrical transmission lines.

What really focused the Scotts' attention was the behavior of the UFO. Whoever, or whatever, was piloting the craft seemed to be very curious about the family. Slowly the UFO hovered, then descended until it seemed to be about one hundred feet overhead. The Scotts estimated that it had a diameter of forty feet. By now extremely apprehensive about their strange observer, the Scotts began packing up their picnic gear.

Then the scary part began. Each family member later reported the same sensation: Time seemed to almost stand still. Their perception of time was that it took on a dreamlike, slow-motion quality. A vivid purple light beamed down on them from the spacecraft.

As the father described it, the light gave the sensation of being a warm, thick liquid. "It felt like warm pancake syrup completely enveloping me," he said. There was no sensation of suffocation or drowning, and afterward, their clothing, skin, and hair were dry. Their wristwatches and cell phones never worked again; apparently they had been affected by strong magnetic fields.

After an estimated half hour, the purple light blinked off, and time began to resume its normal pace in their perception. The UFO slowly ascended to a thousand feet, then accelerated like a NASCAR driver as it disappeared to the south.

The Scotts are convinced that they were subjected to some sort of noninvasive complete body scan. Were the occupants of the UFO on some sort of scientific research mission? The Scotts are sure that was the case. Incidentally, all the food in their picnic basket was gone after the UFO inspection visit. Was that part of the scientific research agenda, or was it just a free lunch for whomever or whatever was inside the UFO? Hope they enjoyed the deviled eggs.

The Ghosts of Bullion Bend

It is not uncommon for modern highways to follow the routes of the old stagecoach roads. So it is with U.S. Route 50 between Carson City, Nevada, and Sacramento. From Lake Tahoe westward through Johnson's Pass, the new road, like the old, passes through some of the most spectacular mountain scenery in the state. Today the road provides access to several ski slopes and summer resorts. In the past, it was traveled by heavy freight wagons bringing supplies to mining camps, covered wagons of emigrants, and stagecoaches. The stagecoaches often were targeted by bandits, as they were known to carry shipments of gold and silver bullion from the mines to Sacramento and on to San Francisco.

At Bullion Bend, about fifteen miles east of Placerville, a stone monument by the roadside commemorates a famous stagecoach robbery—one that involved the Civil War. California was a "Northern" state, loyal to the Union. California was admitted to the union in 1850, and Nevada achieved statehood in 1864. Both were extremely important to the Union's war effort for one simple reason: The gold and silver of these states paid for the war. Not all Californians were enthusiastic about President Lincoln's policies, however.

What happened on June 30, 1864, at Bullion Bend was not a routine holdup; far from it. And this incident in history has provided a local legend of the phantom stagecoaches. To hear old-timers tell it, the ghosts of two stagecoaches and their robbers have been known to reappear on foggy summer mornings. It is as though spirits from a century and a half ago were repeating the dramatic history of Bullion Bend.

A stage labors slowly up the long grade. Its horses, exhausted by pulling a heavy load up a hill, are barely able to move. Suddenly six heavily armed men move out onto the road from the cover of rocks. "Throw down your treasure box!" they command. Three boxes of gold and silver bullion are seized. Just then, a second stage comes around the bend. It too is robbed, this time of four large boxes of California gold and Nevada silver—a true fortune. "Please don't rob the passengers," pleads one driver. "We have no intention of doing so," replies the man evidently heading the team of robbers. "Cooperate and no blood will be spilled." Before galloping off, the polite leader hands each driver a written receipt: "This is to certify that I have received from Wells, Fargo and Company gold and silver bullion for the purpose of recruiting and equipping men enlisted in the Confederate Army. R. Henry Ingrim, Captain, Confederate States of America. June 30, 1864."

Two of the "soldiers" were arrested early the next day; unwisely, they had slept late at a nearby inn. Two others, cornered by a sheriff's posse, shot it out and escaped after killing two men. Another Confederate was captured and hanged at Placerville. No one ever heard of Captain Ingrim again, and no one knows what happened to all that gold and silver captured for the Confederate cause. Maybe the ghosts of Bullion Bend know.

Phantom Steamboat Race

Their great paddle wheels churning furiously, the two riverboats steam up the river in a tightly contested race. The light of a full moon gives their wakes a phosphorescent glow, and sparks fly from their tall, flared twin smokestacks. Passengers line the decks, jeering at their opponent and hoping they'll win the bets they've placed. Sounds like a scene on the Mississippi River, doesn't it? Except that races like this one occurred on the Sacramento River,

and several races here, just like on the Mississippi, ended in fiery disaster.

There are people who swear that every January 27, the ghostly apparitions of two famous stern wheelers, the *Pearl* and the *Enterprise*, appear on the Sacramento River below the city's southern limits. For nearly a century, steamboats competed with one another for the passenger and freight trade between San Francisco and Sacramento. The fastest vessels attracted the most customers, so the competing steamboat lines emphasized speed over safety. Back in the 1850s through 1880s, steamboats were notoriously likely to explode and burn, usually as a result of ignorance and greed. Few then fully understood the awesome pressure within steam boilers. Safety valves, designed to vent unsafe pressure, routinely were tied down or bypassed by engineers ordered to attain greater speed and thus greater profits.

A long list of steamboat catastrophes occurred on San Francisco, San Pablo, and Suisun bays, as well as the Carquinez Strait and Sacramento River. Boats such as the *Washoe*, *Yosemite*, and *Belle* vanished in fiery explosions.

The tragic end of the *Pearl*, which evidently led to its annual ghostly reappearance on the river, resulted in the death of fifty-six people. Catastrophic, grisly deaths often produce ghosts, or at least legends of ghosts. Death aboard the *Pearl* was particularly gruesome and excruciating. The exploding boiler scalded some crew and passengers to death with live steam—in effect, cooking them. Then the smashed furnace sent showers of sparks and red-hot embers through the largely wooden boat, turning it into a floating torch.

Those who claim to have witnessed the tragic reincarnation of the disaster swear they heard the unearthly screams of the *Pearl*'s victims echoing across the river. So if you fear the agonizing cries of the dying, stay away from the Sacramento River on January 27.

Victims of the Curse of Gold

The two ghosts are linked by their histories and similar fates, although their present haunts are nearly thirty-five miles apart. The ghost of Johann Augustus Sutter is said to haunt the restored fort at Sacramento that had been his headquarters. The ghost of James

Marshall, who discovered gold while working for Sutter, appears near his statue at the Marshall Gold Discovery State Historic Park in Coloma.

Both phantoms have this in common: They hang their heads low, their faces reflecting complete dejection. They are beaten men, ruined by their extraordinary bad luck of discovering gold. Yes, bad luck, for when Marshall first spotted those flakes of gold in the gravel and sand of the American River, only disaster followed for both Marshall and Sutter.

Johann, known as John Sutter, had been a captain in the Swiss Army. He wanted to be a farmer and landowner, so he came to Mexican California, having heard that California's climate and fertile soils were far better for farming than those of his native Switzerland. Sutter took Mexican citizenship and acquired from Governor Alvarado a huge land grant of twenty-two square leagues (97,648 acres), which he called New Helvetia (New Switzerland). Sutter built an empire of his own, headquartered in his fort. The fort had walls eighteen feet high and two and a half feet thick. Sutter wanted protection from hostile Indians and also knew that a safe place like his fort would attract traders and settlers who would make him rich. Captain Sutter made his fortune by making a deal with the Russians. Russian explorers had colonized Alaska and came down the Pacific coast as far as Fort Rossiya (Russia), which the locals shortened to Fort Ross. When the Russians conceded to Mexico that they would give up Fort Ross and limit their settlements to Alaska, John Sutter agreed to buy the fort from them. He dismantled many of the buildings and shipped them, as well as 1,700 cattle, 9,000 sheep, and 940 horses, back to New Helvetia. Included in the deal were twelve French cannons captured by the Russians during Napoleon's retreat from Moscow in 1812. Thus it came about that Napoleon's cannon were used by a Swiss Mexican to defend against Indians in California.

Captain Sutter's vast farm employed several hundred men. He ran thirty plows at a time and annually raised forty thousand bushels of wheat, selling much of it to the Russians in Alaska. As Sutter said, "I found a good market for my products among the newcomers [the Americans] and the Russians. My best days were just before the discovery of gold." Then Sutter hired James Marshall to build a sawmill on the American River at Coloma.

When Marshall spotted flakes of gold in the riverbed, he thought his luck had turned. It had—for the worse. First people didn't believe him. Then, when they realized the discovery was genuine, thousands suddenly showed up to look for gold. The hordes of miners, would-be miners, thugs, gunslingers, and crooked judges and lawyers stole and swindled and destroyed Sutter's once-thriving farm enterprise. In disgust and in fear for his life, Captain Sutter left California for the East Coast, never to return. He died a bitter and poor man. James Marshall, his claims scorned by crooked courts, died in poverty within sight of his "lucky" find of gold.

No wonder these two ghosts are disillusioned, ruined men. They both have reason to be sorry that Sutter ever asked Marshall to build a sawmill on the American River. Neither man ever had cause to smile since. Pity their sorrowful ghosts.

The Bloodstained Bridge

As many have learned, to their frustration and regret, bloodstains can be very difficult to remove from any kind of fabric. Blood seems to resist attempts at washing it away. A lot of convicted murderers know how nearly impossible it is to thoroughly obliterate the damning blood evidence from the scene of the crime. In the realm of the supernatural, it seems that bloodstains can persist for decades, even centuries, stubbornly testifying to some past tragedy. Is this blood real, in the physical sense, or is it a psychological stain on the conscience of a murderer or even an entire community?

Many claim to have seen the bloody imprints of hands—many hands, of all sizes, from infants to adults—on the white rocks of a natural bridge formation near Douglas City, a tiny community close to the Whiskeytown–Shasta–Trinity National Recreation Area. The grayish white limestone of the Natural Bridge is said to glisten with a sheen of fresh blood every spring. It is believed that the annual phenomenon commemorates an infamous slaughter of innocents that occurred here in March 1852, which came to be known as the Bridge Gulch Massacre.

The story is that a band of local Wentoon Indians killed a man called Anderson, a prominent citizen of nearby Weaverville. Now, it seems that Anderson was a popular man in town, as he was the bartender at the Golden Horseshoe Saloon. He was a generous man who would serve up a free drink or two when one's gold claim just hadn't paid off yet. When Anderson was brutally beheaded by a war party of Wentoon braves, apparently for no reason other than being in the wrong place at the wrong time, a mob of drunken miners determined to avenge him.

The angry mob descended on a group of about a hundred Indians camped near the Natural Bridge. Every last Indian brave was killed. The miners found women and children huddled fearfully under the bridge and slaughtered them too. Small children were hacked to death with knives when the miners ran out of bullets. It is said that a river of blood flowed under the bridge that day.

As the story goes, one miner was so sickened by the bloodbath that he decided to save the life of one pretty teenage Indian girl. When his friends accused him of being a softhearted traitor to his town, he announced that he had spared her life in order to enslave her. He then sold this lone survivor to a passing teamster for $45, thus restoring his reputation among his friends. So ended the Bridge Gulch Massacre.

Look for the mysterious bloodstains if you visit the Natural Bridge in the springtime.

Come On Down

The widow who told this story wishes to remain anonymous, so we'll call her Susan Miller. Susan and her late husband, Lou, lived in a small, ranch-style house in the suburbs of Sacramento. Susan's encounter with the supernatural was puzzling, but not scary, as it probably saved her life. She wonders still whether the spirit of Lou had come back to warn her of danger, or whether his old chairlift was somehow possessed by a guardian spirit.

Sue and Lou had been empty nesters for some time. Their children had moved far away by the time the elderly couple both retired. Lou had been an insurance broker, while Sue had taught elementary school. While they had an excellent marriage, they each liked some private time alone to pursue their hobbies and interests. Sue converted a spare bedroom into a sewing room, while Lou spent a lot of time handcrafting custom-made dollhouses. Lou's granddaughters each had an elaborate dollhouse, and his creations were highly sought after at the annual church bazaar, as were Sue's hand-embroidered scarves and table covers. Both agreed that their peaceful and harmonious relationship owed much to their each having their private space—which brings us to the chairlift.

Although the house conveniently was a one-story ranch style, it had a large finished basement. The basement woodworking shop was strictly Lou's domain. It was messier than Sue would have liked, so it became a standing joke between them that Sue would visit Lou's basement hobby area by invitation only. In return, he stayed out of her sewing room. Severe degeneration of his knee joints meant that Lou had trouble climbing the stairs to the basement, a problem solved neatly by the installation of a chairlift. The operation of the chairlift, which produced a low whirring sound, was announced in the kitchen by a momentary flickering of the lights, which were on the same electrical circuit as the lift.

A private joke between them was that when Lou wanted Sue to visit his basement kingdom, he would send the chairlift up to the main floor with a plastic flower on the seat. It was, as Lou used to say, her personal engraved invitation to come on down and visit for a while, most likely to admire the progress on his latest project.

Eventually the time came for Lou to join his ancestors, leaving Sue alone in the house. The wood shop in the basement collected dust, as Sue had no reason or desire to go down there anymore. Until the day of the near disaster, that is.

Sue was eating lunch in the kitchen, when the flickering lights indicated that Lou's old chairlift was in motion. Curious, she opened the door to the basement in time to see the chairlift arrive at the top of the stairs. On its seat lay a plastic rose, her "invitation" to come on down. This sent a little shiver down her spine. How could the lift operate itself, and who, or what, had placed the flower on the seat? It was kind of spooky. Hesitantly, she walked down the stairs, ignoring the lift, which she never used anyway. To her consternation, she saw a wisp of smoke curling up from a badly frayed electrical wire connected to Lou's old power jigsaw. Quickly, she unplugged the tool and called the fire department. The fire marshal who checked out the basement for other potential problems told her that in all probability, mice had chewed through the insulation of the electrical cord, causing a short circuit that undoubtedly would have caused a fire—a fire that, feeding on the stock of wood stored nearby, could have rapidly engulfed the house.

If her dead husband's "come on down" message had not led to her timely discovery of the smoking cord, Sue could have lost her house—and possibly her life. The chairlift never again functioned by itself, and Sue regularly checks that all is well in the basement. Did Lou's spirit find a way to communicate from beyond the grave when his beloved was in danger? Sue thinks so.

Stop Calling!

Sometimes justice triumphs at an unofficial and definitely personal level. And in at least one instance, it seems that justice was achieved by supernatural intervention, a very welcome one that was much appreciated by a family in Lodi.

Like most folks, the Reynolds family really disliked those annoying unsolicited phone calls that always seem to come while preparing or eating dinner. The Reynoldses had signed up for the Do Not Call Registry, but there are a lot of annoying loopholes in that law. Religious, political, and charitable organizations can still call, as can any person or company with whom one has ever had any dealings in the past.

Grandpa Reynolds, who had lived with his son's family ever since Grandma had gone to that big bingo game in the sky, was especially irate about unsolicited phone calls. He still remembered the good old days when a ringing phone meant either a welcome call from a friend or, at worst, a mother-in-law who couldn't be ignored safely. Now, it seemed, there was at least a fifty-fifty chance that you did not wish to hear from whoever was calling. Grandpa, who in his younger years was no saint, had grown grouchier and even less patient with age. He'd never suffered fools or foolishness, and now he actually took pleasure from, as he said, "giving the idiots a piece of my mind." Anyone who annoyed him was duly classified as an idiot, and those pieces of his mind were rancorous and abrasive.

When Grandpa answered the phone, which was often, given that he wasn't doing much and was home a lot, unwanted solicitors got a real earful. His family constantly reminded him not to use obscenity over the phone, so he began to devise ingenious means of retaliating against repeat offenders. He caused the unordered delivery of fifteen large, deluxe pizzas—hold the anchovies—to a local business office that phoned at dinnertime despite Grandpa's warning not to call again. The phone company that kept nagging the Reynoldses to switch carriers found its office unexpectedly invaded by the water and sewage department's emergency team, responding to a complaint of a strong smell of sewer gas. The bank that kept calling to try to get the Reynolds family to use its credit card more frequently was visited by the county rodent control officer, following a complaint that the office was overrun by a pack of rats.

As Grandpa lay on his deathbed, he grimly assured his family that his spirit would continue to defend and protect them from those hated, relentless telephone solicitors. "I'll find a way," he promised with his last breath. He was nothing if not righteously vengeful.

The Reynolds family is convinced that Grandpa has indeed found a way to harass the harassers, and that his determined spirit somehow has enlisted allies in the animal kingdom. One offending caller's office was overrun by thousands of big cockroaches. A swarm of bees elected to relocate in the telephone sales department of a big corporation. A large, noisy flock of seagulls decided to hang around another offending office, spattering cars in the employee's parking lot with droppings that etched through the paint. Obnoxious geese laid eggs in the shrubbery outside the entrance to yet another culprit's office, aggressively defending the nest by pinching the ankles and legs of employees black and blue with their beaks. The city advised the company not to harass the geese, a protected species. Sewer rats, skunks, and rabid raccoons made life miserable for other minions of harassment by phone, much to the delight of the Reynoldses.

"Grandpa is still at it," they chuckle as they hear the news. "Good for him." The unsolicited calls have definitely diminished. Justice at last.

The Miner's Curse

For well over a century now, some really strange things have been happening at the Snowball Mansion Inn in Knights Landing. This popular, elegant bed-and-breakfast inn was built in the 1870s by a wealthy man named John Snowball. John had the mansion built as a wedding present for his beautiful bride, Lucy. Knights Landing, in those days, was a flourishing port on the Sacramento River northwest of Sacramento, and Snowball was the richest man in town.

John was handsome and rich, Lucy young, intelligent, and lovely. Their future seemed bright. When Lucy became pregnant, the couple rejoiced that their world was complete. Life was beautiful and fulfilling. What could go wrong?

The French novelist Balzac once said, "Behind every great fortune there is a crime." If not generally true, it was in John Snowball's case. He made a lot of money as a merchant supplying goods to miners, cowboys, and farmers. A shrewd judge of character, John would extend credit at his store to miners on their way to the Sierra goldfields. The miners, eager to get to the gold country to try their luck, would agree in writing to share their strike, if any, with Snowball. The fine print on these contracts included an interest rate that even the Mafia loan sharks would have considered a tad exorbitant.

It is said that one of the ambitious miners who signed Snowball's contracts was a Welshman named Jones. Now, the Welsh name Jones came from the biblical name Jonah. As students of the Bible know, Jonah is a symbol of the calamitous consequences of questioning God's will. Anyone named Jones, in Welsh folklore, is capable of cursing others with bad luck.

When William Jones returned to Knights Landing with a little sack of gold nuggets, he felt rich indeed. He had made a small fortune. He owed John Snowball 50 percent of his gold in payment for his supplies. So he gave John half of the gold. "Thanks, but you also owe interest on the loan," reminded John. "Interest?" said a newly apprehensive Jones. "Yes, 10 percent interest on $100 worth of supplies. Ten percent a week times the fifteen weeks you've been gone—that's 150 percent interest, thank you very much," said John as he took another handful of gold.

"Damn you to hell!" yelled Jones. "You've taken most of my hard-earned gold!" John Snowball just laughed. As he stomped away, the infuriated Jones added to the curse: "And damn your seed!"

In due time, Lucy gave birth to a healthy, handsome little boy named John Jr., known as Jack. Jack was a dear and seemed to flourish—at first. Then, tragically, Jack stopped eating. He rapidly dropped weight. The doctors could do nothing. Little Jack died at the age of three months.

Legend has Jones attending little Jack's funeral. "I hope you've enjoyed the gold you cheated me of," he told John Snowball, "but now you are impoverished in your heart through the loss of your son." Unhinged by grief, John Snowball committed suicide a week later. Lucy, having lost her child and husband, fell into a deep depression from which she never recovered. She lived as a recluse in her mansion for the rest of her life.

Lucy's profound sense of loss evidently has caused her spirit to remain in her house. Some have reported seeing her misty figure walking the hallways, carrying a wailing infant that she tries to comfort. Her ghost passes through a wall where the door to the nursery once was. Sometimes her voice can be heard in the one-time nursery singing lullabies to her doomed child. Windows rattle as her spirit passes by, and dishes fly off tables and smash. Apparently poor Lucy is still suffering from the terrible curse laid on her husband by the angry Welsh miner Jones.

Outrunning the Devil

Old-timers around Yuba City still remember the story of the haunted house and the traveling preacher. The incident happened so long ago that many of the details are a little fuzzy by now.

It seems that in the 1860s, an itinerant preacher was traveling from Sacramento to the mining camps in the foothills of the Sierra—places like Grass Valley, Nevada City, and Rough and Ready, which sounded as though it could really use a preacher. In those days, it was customary for Methodist clergy to "ride the circuit," i.e. travel to remote communities to preach, perform weddings and baptisms, and generally bring the word of God to places too small to have a permanent church. They relied on the hospitality of strangers for shelter and food as they made their way across the countryside.

Reverend Sam, as he liked to be called, was on the road south of Yuba City when an autumn storm caught up with him at dusk. He stopped at a remote farmhouse, introduced himself, and politely asked if he might spend the night. "Well, now! I hate to turn you down, Preacher, we being Christian folks," said the farmer, "but our large family already is sleeping two to a bed, and we just don't have any room. You are welcome to join us for supper, and we'd appreciate your baptizing our youngest, born four months ago. There is an empty house just up the road where you could spend the night—it's fully furnished, but no one wants it because it is said to be haunted by Satan himself. But you being a minister of the gospel, maybe you'd be safe."

There was a hint of challenge to the farmer's account of the haunted house. How could a self-respecting man of the cloth admit he was afraid of meeting evil? Reverend Sam performed the requested baptism, enjoyed a good dinner, and set out for the empty house.

As the farmer had said, the house was in good repair and equipped with furniture, including a large, invitingly soft bed. There was a stack of firewood beside the fireplace and even a jug of fresh spring water on the table. Reverend Sam lit a fire and settled into a comfortable easy chair in front of the fireplace. He took the precaution of placing his Bible on his lap and, after removing his boots, began to doze off.

Suddenly the reverend's eyes snapped open to behold a large, handsome rooster perched on a chair opposite him. It was covered in glossy black feathers with dark green highlights. With his bright red comb and yellow and black eyes, the rooster was quite a sight. "And who might you be?" asked the rooster in a clear baritone. "I'm Reverend Sam, a Methodist circuit rider, and I'm not afraid of whoever or whatever you might be" was his reply. "Well, as you may have guessed, I'm that fallen angel you warn people about in your sermons—I'm Satan himself!" said the rooster. The bird flew abruptly at the reverend, his sharp beak aimed at the man's eyes. Reverend Sam quickly raised his Bible to fend off the attack, and the rooster disappeared in a puff of foul-smelling smoke.

Next, a small black kitten showed up and crawled over Reverend Sam's stocking feet. As Sam watched, the kitten grew into a large, aggressive tomcat. "I've decided to convert you to Satanism," growled the cat. "I'm sure I can convince you to worship me, and don't even think about trying to leave. I've had the door nailed shut."

Sam dove through the window and began running as if the Devil were after him, which was all too true. The big cat followed and sneered, "I'll catch up to you—you can't run very far without your boots on!" Remembering the folktales about the Devil not being able to cross running water, Sam plunged into a small stream. Sure enough, the frustrated cat inhabited by Satan stopped abruptly at the water's edge. Reverend Sam survived his encounter with Satan but learned an important lesson that all mortals should take to heart: When in a haunted house, keep your boots or shoes on—you might need to outrun the Devil.

Boo!

Boo was a real character. Everyone who had known him agreed on that. Now that he had gone to cat heaven, his ghost was a real character and psychic too, if the stories about him are to be believed.

Boo had come into Aunt Mary's life the usual way—a friend had pleaded with her to take a kitten from her cat's litter. Not that it took a lot of persuading, as the tiny kitten, which was all black except for a white blaze on his throat, had been his own best salesman with his lovable and outgoing personality.

At first he had been called Baby, but maturity and an unusual habit earned a name change to Boo. Boo liked to surprise people, both his owner and any visitors. He would approach silently and just out of sight if possible. Then, boo! He would leap suddenly onto a lap and go nose-to-nose, his bright yellow eyes staring boldly into the eyes of his human host. He seemed to enjoy the sometimes startled reaction to his dramatic appearance.

It was Boo's seemingly supernatural abilities that really impressed Aunt Mary, and later her niece. Boo predeceased Aunt Mary by only a few weeks. Mary left her small house in Sacramento to her niece Alice, a bequest that included Boo's spirit, along with his uncanny ability to foretell the immediate future.

Boo hadn't lived with Mary very long before she realized that he knew, just knew, when bad news was coming. Now, Boo was not a particularly vocal cat, not like his predecessor, a Burmese. Boo rarely gave voice to his feelings, except a polite meow or two as a reminder that it was approaching dinnertime.

Boo's first premonition of trouble came late one night. Mary was in bed sound asleep, when Boo suddenly crept up on the bed, thudding onto her chest. "Yowl!" he went. "Rowl, rowl!" Mary woke up to find herself nose to nose with her visibly agitated cat. Soon after, the phone rang. It was terrible news: A close friend had been killed in a car crash. But Mary was convinced that Boo's midnight visit to her had preceded the phone call by a few minutes. He had never awakened her like that before. How had Boo known that bad news was imminent? Did he have some sort of feline radar, detecting a threat to his mistress's happiness and composure, minutes before the bad news reached her?

There followed a number of other instances of Boo's early warning of tragedy. On several occasions, Boo would run to the telephone and stare at it, body rigid, tail twitching, fur upright along his spine, and loudly meow just before a phone call with sad news. "Boo is psychic!" Mary would say. "It's a little scary."

After both Boo and Aunt Mary had departed this world, Alice moved into the house she'd inherited. It soon became clear that she'd also inherited Boo, or at least his spirit.

Was it just a nightmare, or did Boo awaken Alice from an afternoon nap by jumping up on her? Thud! A large, somewhat overweight tomcat leaping up on one certainly interrupts sleep. Did she imagine it, or were two greenish-yellow eyes an inch from hers as she awakened? No, that couldn't be—or could it? Just then, the phone rang. A cousin tearfully announced a medical diagnosis of inoperable cancer. The cat's spirit had known. Boo!

The Ghost of the Godfather

The obese ghost walks slowly down the grand staircase of the elegant Victorian mansion. He is dressed in a beautifully tailored three-piece suit with a gold-embroidered vest, a red silk tie, and a heavy gold watch chain stretched across his impressive stomach. He flashes a broad, welcoming smile just before his image fades away. You have just met the phantom of one of California's most influential men, one who shaped the early state through his political powers and influence, as well as his vast fortune. The spirit of Leland Stanford is believed to haunt his Sacramento mansion, which he donated to the state and is now a combination museum and venue for official meetings and receptions. The Leland Stanford Mansion Historic Park served as the official residence of three governors back in the 1860s, starting with Governor Stanford.

Leland Stanford, who was born in New York in 1824, decided to join his five brothers in California in 1852. A shrewd businessman, he opened a store in Sacramento with his brother and made a fortune selling supplies to gold miners. When the state's Democratic party split over the slavery issue, he ran for governor as a Republican and won in 1861. He worked hard to keep California in the Union, and the state's gold helped finance the Civil War. His magnificent mansion was built in 1856 and expanded in 1872. It was the site of a lot of lobbying to persuade California, and the federal government, to finance the building of a transcontinental railroad linking the state with the East Coast. Stanford understood that only such a railroad would enable California to reach its full potential.

Along with fellow millionaires Collis Huntington, Mark Hopkins, and Charles Crocker, Stanford organized the Central Pacific Railroad. They built eastward from Sacramento across the High Sierra and on to Promontory Point, Utah, where their tracks met those of the Union Pacific, building westward from Omaha, in 1869.

The success of the transcontinental railroad made Stanford much richer. He had been educated as a lawyer and was very interested in politics all his life. He was especially interested in what government could do to make him richer. Although he served only one term as governor, he had a lot of political influence. His Central Pacific Railroad merged into the Southern Pacific, which became known as the "octopus" because it controlled the state's economy.

Stanford considered himself to be a hardheaded businessman. Many would have used a different vocabulary—ruthless, manipulative, greedy, exploitative, and much worse. But then Leland Stanford had a psychic experience that transformed his life.

One night, his only child, Leland Jr., appeared to him in a dream—a very unsettling dream. Junior announced that he was dead. His spirit begged his father to use some of his vast wealth to benefit society. "Do good in my memory," asked the spirit. The next morning, Stanford got a telegram from Europe. It notified him that his sixteen-year-old son had died of typhoid while on an educational tour of the continent.

To honor his dead son, Stanford donated a large Santa Clara Valley ranch, together with a huge endowment, to found Leland Stanford Junior University. During his time as a U.S. senator, from 1885 to his death in 1893, Stanford generally was regarded as "undistinguished"—political-speak for lazy and unimaginative—except for one idea: He was almost alone in championing the idea that the federal government should support public education with tax money. The senator was about eighty years ahead of his time on that issue. Stanford believed that only universal access to quality education would eliminate racial differences in income and status. He knew it was the right thing to do, he said, because his dead son told him so.

Leland Stanford's ghost, like the man himself, must be an interesting combination of positive and negative energies—an unprincipled, ruthless, greedy businessman and a generous, farsighted benefactor. You might smile back should you meet the spirit of Leland Stanford. In many ways, he was the founder, the godfather of the state of California.

North Coast

THE NORTH COAST REGION STRETCHES FROM THE GOLDEN GATE northward to the Oregon border and includes the coast ranges of mountains. This three-hundred-mile-long region includes the enormous coast redwoods and the world-famous wine country of the Napa and Sonoma Valleys. Important cities include Santa Rosa, Novato, and Eureka. Along this often foggy coast, with its neighboring scenic mountains and valleys filled with vineyards, you will encounter a fascinating variety of ghosts and other paranormal phenomena, including the gentle spirit of a scientific wizard, the ghost of a poet who also robbed stagecoaches, the phantoms of the victims of a shipwreck, and the specters of some frustrated and angry Native Americans. Adding to the variety of the supernatural landscape, Northern California is part of Bigfoot country, and the region also may have played host to ancient invasions of UFOs.

Ask the Magic Mountain

Native American lore contains several stories in which the spirits of dying people take on a new physical expression as a landmark. Traditionally, great and powerful individuals are transformed into mountains; such is held to be the case with forty-two-hundred-foot-high Mount Konochti.

Mount Konochti is very special to a small group of believers who are convinced that the mountain has magical powers and can predict the future. This mountain is particularly accurate, they claim, at seeing the future of lovers and thus giving good advice to those looking for a long-lasting, "made in heaven" relationship.

The tradition is that many years ago, when the earth was young, the Pomo Indians lived on islands in Clear Lake and used great rafts to ferry themselves among the islands and to the lake's shores. The mighty and wise chief of the Pomo was Konochti, and he had a lovely young daughter, Lupiyomi. One day a rival chief, Kahbel, came to Konochti asking for Lupiyomi's hand in marriage. Konochti firmly refused. It was not in the stars that this would be a happy marriage. The two would-be partners were not truly compatible; they came from different tribes and had different values. Physical attraction alone would not be the basis for a lasting union.

Kahbel, driven by pride and lust, attempted to kidnap Lupiyomi. The two chiefs, accompanied by their warriors, clashed on the shores of Clear Lake. Kahbel had supernatural powers, which he used in attempting to build a causeway to the island on which Lupiyomi dwelt. This narrow spit of land, which almost cuts Clear Lake in two, can be seen to this day. At the narrows, as this tongue of land is now called, Konochti and Kahbel fought it out, using magical powers to hurl enormous boulders at one another. These huge rocks, the size of small cars, can be seen on surrounding mountain slopes to this day. Kahbel was killed and Konochti mortally wounded. As Konochti was dying, the spirits transformed his soul into the majestic mountain that bears his name.

Some believe that the spirit of Chief Konochti dwells within his mountain, ever ready to advise lovers on their compatibility and long-term prospects as a couple. It is said that if both lovers stand together on the shores of Clear Lake and earnestly ask for the chief's advice as they face Mount Konochti, they will get their answer twenty-four hours later. If the sun shines on the mountain, the answer is yes—you will be a happy couple for eternity. If fog or mist obscures the peak, then Konochti is advising the couple to further explore their relationship before making a decision. But if storm clouds appear over the mountain, the couple will have a similarly stormy future and should seek other mates. If a large boulder on the mountain dislodges itself and tumbles down the slope, this proposed union could end in murder. Many scoff at the idea of the magic mountain giving advice to courting couples. On the other hand, a lot more than one couple wish they had listened to Konochti's warning.

The Shipwrecked Spirits

Old-timers in the vicinity of Crescent City repeat the story of the mysterious campfires on the beaches. Many believe that these fires, and the shadowy figures gathered around them, commemorate a famous shipwreck of long ago.

Crescent City was named for its harbor, defined by a crescent-shaped beach. The harbor, which came to be a supply center and port for gold mining in the neighborhood, is protected from the strong north winds along this coast by Point St. George, a rocky headland projecting out to sea. While the promontory of Point St. George offers shelter, St. George Reef, a rocky ledge just offshore, offers death and destruction—a sort of evil twin. St. George Reef is a barely submerged seaward continuation of the same rocks that form the point. If ships heading for the sheltered waters of Crescent City come a little too close to the point, they end up in the jagged jaws of St. George Reef.

That is what happened on July 30, 1865. The side-wheeler *Brother Jonathan* was blown onto the reef by a fierce summer storm. Grounded in the rocks, the ship was helpless, unmaneuverable. Steadily, it was pounded to pieces by the heavy surf, its passengers and crew paralyzed by terror at their fate. They could see, by the light of a half-moon, Point St. George and the little port lined up along the sweeping curve of the harbor. So near, and yet so far! *Brother Jonathan*'s lifeboats were smashed into splinters by the great waves breaking on the reef. Escape from the foundering ship was impossible. One by one, people were swept off the decks to certain death in the surging currents, bashed against the rocks or drowned in the frigid sea.

Local legend has it that later that evening, the dead bodies, which had washed ashore, gathered around a great bonfire built on the beach out of driftwood. There are two theories as to the meaning and purpose of the first fire, and the annual re-creations, on the beach. Some believe that the ghosts of the dead somehow built a fire by which they could warm their lifeless bodies once more before moving on to the realm of the spirits. Souls brave enough to approach the mysterious bonfires that spring up on the beach every July 30 have reported seeing the phantoms of shipwrecked corpses gathered about the fire. Their sodden clothing steams as seawater evaporates from them, and strands of seaweed cling to their lifeless forms.

An alternative explanation for the fires is that they are impromptu, makeshift lighthouses set up by the dead spirits to warn other ships away from St. George Reef. Maybe the ghostly fires serve both purposes.

Incidentally, you can still visit the graves of many of the victims of the *Brother Jonathan* tragedy at the Brother Jonathan Cemetery at Ninth Street and Pebble Beach Drive. It might be a good idea, however, to avoid the cemetery on the night of July 30. There is no telling who—or what—you might encounter.

The Gentleman Bandit's Ghost

Normally, meeting the spirit of a notorious robber would be a fearsome occasion. Highway robbers, in person or in spirit, are usually pretty scary. The ghost of one particular stagecoach robber, however, is the picture of politeness and can be a charming phantom indeed.

The ghost of the famous bandit Black Bart has been known to appear at Black Bart Rock, a landmark alongside Highway 101 about ten miles south of the town of Willits. Black Bart's spirit wears his trademark elegantly tailored black suit, white shirt with black tie, black hat, well-polished black boots—and a black mask, for Black Bart never showed his face. He robbed more than thirty stages in Northern California between 1875 and 1883. Bart always was immaculately dressed and invariably polite. He never took personal jewelry from his victims and never injured or shot anyone. His "requests" for money, backed up by a Colt revolver, were accompanied by "please if you will" and "thank you kindly." While staging a robbery, he liked to talk in rhymes. After emptying the express boxes of money, he would leave behind a little card with a poem signed, "Black Bart, Poet." His poems often were humorous, and he never made a spelling or grammatical error.

Black Bart might never have been caught if not for his habit of sending his clothes out to a laundry. During his final holdup, a woman passenger in the stagecoach burst into tears from the stress of being held at gunpoint. Black Bart gallantly gave her his fresh linen handkerchief. Police found a laundry mark on the handkerchief and traced it to a San Francisco cleaner. Eventually the linen was traced to one Charles C. Bolton, a respectable middle-class family man. Bolton had been educated as a mining engineer and told his family that his frequent trips out of town were visits to mines.

Black Bart was sentenced to two years in San Quentin, where he read and wrote poetry. On his release, he resumed his old career as a mining engineer and never committed another crime. But it seems that his spirit still pursues his alternative job as a stagecoach robber—or at least tries to, despite a real scarcity of stagecoaches on Highway 101 these days.

The Wizard of Santa Rosa

The tall, slightly stooped figure looks like an unexpected blend of a distinguished professional man—perhaps a doctor or lawyer—and a gardener. He is dressed in a conservative, pinstriped three-piece suit, complete with white shirt and silk tie. But he also is wearing a bib apron, which shows splotches of damp earth and a collection of old stains. The apron's deep pockets hold the tools of the professional gardener—trowels, dirt forks, and pruning knives. Carefully, he expertly prepares a young seedling to receive a twig to be grafted onto it. Looking up, he gives the visitor a rather distracted smile, then returns to his work, totally absorbed in his efforts. If approached too closely, the gentleman simply disappears, for he was never really there except in a spiritual sense. You have just met the ghost of Luther Burbank, who fittingly haunts the gardens and greenhouse at his former home in Santa Rosa, now a museum.

Many visitors have spotted Burbank's spirit on the grounds of his house and assumed that they were looking at an impersonator, a museum guide costumed to play the role of the great horticulturist himself. The museum staff denies that any such impersonator ever was employed. The ghost of Luther Burbank simply is doing what the living man did best—working with nature to create new and improved varieties of plants for the enjoyment of everyone.

Luther Burbank had a very strong, productive compulsion in life—to work with plants, blending and combining their desirable traits into what he called "new creations." He worked long and diligently in his greenhouse and gardens, constantly experimenting with cross-pollination and grafting to "speed up," as he put it, nature's evolution of new varieties of plants, even totally new plants. Burbank was not particularly interested in scientific theories. He saw himself as a kind of inventor, a tinkerer with living plants.

He came to the Sonoma Valley from Worcester, Massachusetts, in 1875 at the age of twenty-six. He had already decided on a career as a plant breeder and considered this part of California to be perfect for plant experimentation. He wrote of the Santa Rosa area, "I firmly believe from what I have seen that it is the chosen spot of all this earth as far as nature is concerned." During his fifty years living in Santa Rosa, Burbank created more than eight hundred new varieties of plants, including sixty types of plums and prunes. His achievements include the Burbank potato, Santa Rosa plum, Burbank cherry, and a new fruit, the plumcot, a plum and apricot mix. In addition to his delicious contributions to the food supply, Burbank created new varieties of flowers to "feed the soul as well as the stomach"—Shasta daisies, Peachblow roses, and fragrant calla lilies. He worked, too, on developing edible cactus and improved types of asparagus and tomatoes.

Maybe if you are lucky enough to encounter his benign ghost, you could quietly suggest he work on biofuels; he'd probably like that. You can visit his home and gardens at the corner of Santa Rosa and Sonoma avenues. Enjoy, and watch for his spirit still "tinkering" with his beloved plants.

A Most Helpful Ghost

According to students of the supernatural, many ghost stories fall into one of a number of categories—types of spirits grouped by their behavior, manner of death, or motivation. One such category is called "guardian ghosts." These apparitions appear to the living in an attempt to warn them of danger or protect them from harm. Frequently, they are the spirits of persons who, in life, were dedicated to serve and protect. Police officers, firefighters, and military personnel seem to frequently become, in death, guardian ghosts. In a sense, they are still on duty, honoring their life commitment.

The little town of Bodega Bay has such a guardian ghost. The bay is too shallow for large vessels, so the community has specialized in sportfishing, with "party boats" and individually owned small craft. The town's chief claim to fame is as the setting of Alfred Hitchcock's classic 1963 horror film *The Birds*.

Bodega Bay's guardian spirit is said to be that of a sweet-natured, mildly mentally challenged man who died half a century ago. No one remembers his given name, as everyone called him Helpful. Having been told many times that he was helpful, he began introducing himself simply as Helpful, and the nickname stuck. Helpful made himself a fixture in the little town by his willingness to tackle any chore for anyone. He would clean and polish small boats for their owners, wash and wax cars, serve as a mate on party boats, and gut and scale the catch for successful fishermen. A local restaurant and bar let him sleep on a cot in a storeroom in return for his janitorial services.

One of Helpful's most endearing qualities was that he was a baseball fanatic. He excitedly watched every game on the bar's television, and his childlike enthusiasm was contagious. Having memorized all the baseball statistics back to Babe Ruth, he could reel off team and career data with unerring accuracy. He settled many a bar bet and never made a mistake.

Perhaps thanks to his hanging around pleasure craft so much at the marina, he was in the habit of addressing any male over the age of fourteen as "Captain." Helpful had a sixth sense about the weather; he was uncannily accurate about storms at sea that had not been predicted by professional weather forecasts. "I don't think you want to go out today, Captain; there's going to be a sudden squall out there today," he'd advise boat owners. His predictions were invariably true, and everyone listened to Helpful. When he died of pneumonia, the community chipped in to give him a decent burial. To this day, his friendly ghost appears on the docks to warn, "Don't go out today, Captain; it's going to be rough."

The Spirits of the Ghost Dancers

The ghostly figures of as many as one hundred Native Americans are formed into a great circle. Each dancer's arms resting on the shoulders of his neighbors, the dancers shuffle slowly to their left. Sometimes the infamous ghost dance, as it is called, continues with this slow, almost hypnotic movement until the participants gradually drop out from exhaustion. On other, much more threatening occasions, the dance becomes progressively faster until the dancers are whirling about frantically. In this variant, the dancers' faces seem frozen in a trance, and unlike the monotonous rhythm of the slow shuffle, the dance climaxes in a frenzy of writhing, twisting action. Loud shouting accompanies this hyperactive version of the ghost dance.

The ghost dance was brought from Washington State to Klamath, a small town on California's north coast, in the 1860s by an Indian named Jimmie Jacks. He, in turn, had learned it from Smohalla, chief of the Columbia River Indians. Smohalla, the story goes, had blended his interpretation of Christian teachings with traditional Indian lore, proclaiming himself the new Messiah. By dancing the ghost dance, he claimed, Native Americans would once again rule the American West. Indian dead would rise up and repopulate the land. A great volcano would pour out a tide of white-hot lava that would incinerate the white men and nonbelieving Indians.

Any Indian could be spared this death by molten lava by dancing the ghost dance. The ghost dancers were to wear magical shirts that would stop a white man's bullet. The dance spread quickly among the western tribes and led to the final spasms of Indian wars, as thousands rose up to try to defeat the whites who were taking their land.

As recently as the 1930s, the ghost dance was being performed at a small church in the town of Klamath. There are many who swear that the spirits of the Indian dead still rise up to do the ghost dance in remote redwood groves to this very day. Unless you happen to be of Native American ancestry, it would not be a good idea to be caught observing a ghostly ghost dance. The spirits are still bitterly vengeful against the whites who drove them from their land. Wouldn't you agree that the ghost dancers had ample reason to seek a new millennium free of oppression? Beware the spirits of the ghost dance.

An Encounter with Bigfoot

Don't ask Marsha Smith if she believes in Bigfoot—she'll repeat a story that will scare your socks off. Marsha, whose real last name is not Smith, lives near the small town of Orrick, which is nearly surrounded by Redwood National Park. Whereas some people claiming to have encountered Bigfoot go public with their story and seem to relish media attention, others tell their tales reluctantly to only select friends, sometimes waiting until years after the event. They just don't want to be thought of as easily fooled, mentally unbalanced, or worse. Marsha fits into this latter category of observers; she wished to avoid controversy and notoriety.

It was a very dark night at Marsha's isolated house, the kind of night when the wind howls through the trees and the moon and stars are hidden behind dense rain clouds rolling in from the sea. It was the sort of night when Marsha, recently widowed and living alone, was glad she had Adolf for company and protection.

Adolf was a rottweiler, a breed recommended to Marsha as a good watchdog. It had been named after the German dictator because of its aggressiveness toward strangers. In truth, however, Adolf was a much nicer dog than Adolf Hitler was a man. "Actually, he's a pussycat around me," Marsha told friends. Loyal and affectionate as the dog was to Marsha, his loud bark and menacing, throaty growl could freeze even police officers in their tracks.

As the rain beat against the house that night, Marsha glanced up quickly at a growl from Adolf, and caught a quick glimpse of two brightly glowing red eyes staring at her through a window. Adolf went berserk, barking and pawing at the backdoor as though the Devil himself were outside. Fearful that the dog would plunge through a window in his excitement, Marsha opened the door for him. Adolf charged out into the yard like a furry rocket.

What happened next was burned into Marsha's memory. She could hear Adolf barking furiously, along with another low-pitched bellowing or growling sound. A lightning flash briefly illuminated a terrifying sight: Adolf was courageously attacking a humanlike form covered in coarse, black hair and standing more than seven feet tall. No sooner had the intense darkness returned than she heard a single high-pitched yelp from Adolf, followed by silence.

Dawn and the police arrived at about the same time. The dog's body lay thirty feet from the house. Not only was his neck broken, but his skull had been crushed like an eggshell. The ground around the dead dog had been churned up by all the action, but huge footprints showed in the soft mud. Before the prints could be cast in plaster, however, another heavy rainfall destroyed them.

The official police report said that this was an attack by a bear, but Marsha doesn't accept that. "I've seen plenty of bears, and this was no bear. The eyes that stared in my window were too big and too closely spaced to be a bear's," she emphasized. "And the creature I saw struggling with Adolf during the lightning flash was no bear."

Bigfoot, or Sasquatch, as it's called in the Pacific Northwest, has been observed by hundreds of people, according to published reports. It is likely that hundreds, if not thousands, more have caught a quick glimpse of the creature but decided not to expose themselves to ridicule by reporting it or allowed themselves to be persuaded that they had actually sighted a bear or moose. The Indians of the Northwest Coast tell legends about Sasquatch, which has led some scientists to conclude that it is a purely mythical creature. But the Indian mythology also includes tales of bears and wolves, which certainly are real.

Many people believe, mistakenly, that apelike animals are strictly tropical, and therefore Bigfoot could not be a primate living so far from the equator. Though there is general agreement that most animal species probably originated in the humid tropics, many have spread successfully into much cooler latitudes. The Siberian tiger and polar bear are good examples. A principle in biology known as Bergmann's rule maintains that animals tend to get bigger the farther they are from the equator, because their greater body mass helps keep them from freezing. Alaskan Kodiak and polar bears, for example, are much larger than their more southerly cousins. Thus it is not surprising that Sasquatch or Bigfoot would be taller than gorillas, chimps, or orangutans.

As many have pointed out, if there is one Bigfoot, there must be thousands—enough to form a breeding population. Is there enough food for Bigfoot in the coastal redwood areas of Northern California? Sure, keeping in mind that often primates, such as chimpanzees, are omnivorous—that is, they eat both plants and animals, as do bears.

Many are convinced that not only are Sasquatches possible, but they do exist. Keep a sharp eye out when driving the backroads of redwood country. You just might spot a Bigfoot.

Mysterious Lights

There are two possible explanations for the twin lights; take your pick. Of course, either story requires that you believe in ghosts.

The house, built in the early 1900s, stands atop a cliff near the town of Arcata. The structure offers a clear view of the Pacific Ocean, and naturally, ships just offshore have an equally good view of the house.

A peculiarity of the house is that in the attic windows are a mysterious pair of lights that never go out, at least not for long. The house had been in one family's possession for three generations, handed down from father to son to grandson. It was only when strangers took it over that anyone noticed the lights—or, rather, the unusual nature of the lights.

The new owners, whom we'll call the Harpers, had seen the house only in daylight before they bought it. Soon after moving in, they were returning to their house one evening when they saw twin lights shining in each of two attic windows, which were about fifteen feet apart. The lights appeared to be quite bright, a slightly greenish white that likely could be seen for a good distance at sea. Neither husband nor wife had left on any lights in the attic; indeed, they had only peeked briefly inside to estimate the storage potential.

Climbing up the steep attic stairs, the couple found the lights, almost hidden from view behind very dusty empty cardboard boxes. The bulbs were powerful floodlamps but were strangely cool to the touch. The lights had no on-off switches and were wired into the house current, so there was no easy way to extinguish them. The couple unscrewed the bulbs and forgot about the whole situation until two nights later, when they again happened to notice the lights shining, bright as ever. Up to the attic they went, finding the bulbs firmly screwed into their sockets. This time, they not only unscrewed the bulbs, but carried them both downstairs and deposited them in the trash.

By now the Harpers were getting a little rattled by the lights that wouldn't be put out. When they checked the next evening, sure enough, the lights again shone. The following day, an electrician who was called in to look at their problem swore that the circuit breaker controlling the attic wiring had frozen in the off position. There was no way electricity could be reaching the attic, "No juice, no lights," he promised as he disconnected the attic line.

But the lights were back on that same night. The Harpers decided to find out why the lights shone instead of focusing on how they worked. A retired sea captain in town thought he knew why there were two lights. "It's an old mariner's trick," he explained. "They are navigational aids. You spot the two lights from out at sea. You adjust your angle of approach to shore until the two lights appear to merge, and that angle of approach will lead you safely through off-shore rocks." Evidently the lights were intended to bring boats in safely to a small cove at the foot of the old house. But why would boats head for the little cove instead of the nearby port of Arcata?

Two stories were supplied by old-timers in the vicinity. One was that the house had belonged to a seafaring family who had lost a son at sea. The missing man's mother had sworn to keep the twin lights burning to guide his spirit safely home. The other story, less romantic but perhaps more widely believed, dated to the days of Prohibition. It seems that the householder was involved in smuggling good Canadian whiskey, which was brought into the secluded cove by small fishing boats. A particularly valuable shipment due to arrive one stormy winter night never arrived. The smuggler boss swore that the twin beacons would shine every night until his boat arrived, even if, he promised, it took an eternity.

Either way, the lights may be of supernatural origin. Still they shine every night, symbols of promises made long ago.

The Dance of Death

The war drums throb incessantly late into the night. The shadows of many warriors dance around the campfire on the beach, but it is not a celebration dance—it is a grimly determined dance of war and vengeance. Woe to any living person who might chance to witness this ghostly ceremony, at least if they are white, for this annual supernatural event commemorates a bloody massacre.

The unprovoked mass murder that instigated the war dance took place on the evening of February 25, 1860. This attack was just one incident in the struggle between the area's earlier inhabitants and the white invaders. The Native American population had declined under Spanish and Mexican rule by more than a third. Under American governance, it declined at a faster rate, falling by at least fifty thousand between 1849 and 1856 alone. This catastrophic drop produced a fundamental split in attitude within the tribes: Should they accept conquest as inevitable and peacefully relocate on the reservations set up for them, or should they fight? Some chose to resist, and a long, intermittent war followed, with attacks and reprisals flickering on and off.

It was this poisoned atmosphere of mutual mistrust and bloodshed that led to the atrocity on Indian Island, which lay in Humboldt Bay south of Eureka. A band of settlers had decided on a preemptive strike—"get them before they get us." Through good intelligence or good luck, the whites had chosen an advantageous time to attack. All the able-bodied Native American men had left their Indian Island camp on a hunting expedition. Women, children, and the tribe's elderly and infirm remained, and these were slaughtered by the whites. The husbands, fathers, and brothers returned on February 25 to find burned homes and mutilated corpses.

The enraged warriors took a blood oath of vengeance and began their war dance—a dance of death. Months of bitter warfare followed. Indian Island eventually was purchased by a man named Gunther, who called it Gunther Island. He built dikes to protect his island from encroaching salt water and took up farming.

Legend has it that Gunther was thoroughly frightened by the annual war dance by phantom warriors on the anniversary of the infamous massacre. He became so fearful of these hostile and threatening ghosts that he decided to abandon his island to the spirits. He destroyed his protective dikes, allowing the waters of the bay to pour over the island, reducing it to salt marsh barely above water at high tide.

Still, every February 25, people claim to hear the drums beat out their message of vengeance and death. Stay clear of the southern end of Humboldt Bay on that night.

An Adventurous Spirit

This particular phantom is seldom seen these days, perhaps indicating that his restless spirit has at last found peace, or at least become resigned to its fate in the next world. Those who report having seen this spirit materialize, however, invariably describe it as full of restless energy, a ghost that, like the once-living person, has a well-developed sense of adventure. This ghost doesn't glide slowly about or stand still, as many phantoms are described. Oh no, this one strides purposefully across the land as though in a hurry. It even has been seen riding an equally ghostly horse, galloping along recklessly as though in search of excitement and adventure. This, onlookers agree, can only be the ghost of Jack London, the early-twentieth-century author who was one of California's most famous native sons.

London's ghost appears infrequently today at his onetime ranch house and gravesite, both located in what is now Jack London State Historic Park near the tiny community of Glen Ellen. His ranch in the Sonoma Valley lies in the heart of the state's wine country and still attracts visitors interested in the life and works of one of America's most popular writers.

In life, London was an adventurous spirit. The great popularity of his books was based on two facts: He was a gifted natural storyteller, and he had wonderful stories to tell, all based on his life experiences. One critic observed that he was his own most interesting character.

Jack's mother was a spiritualist who, by her own admission, was not a very attentive or loving parent. His father rejected his son and would have nothing to do with him, possibly doubting that he was the actual father. Jack's mother's second husband adopted him and gave him his family name, but little else in a family sense. Jack entered the world of rough, heavy, strenuous labor at the age of fourteen and never stopped working. He was a classic workaholic—the sweatier the work, the better. Every job he ever held provided adventures, plots, characters, and settings for his many books.

He started his working life as an "oyster pirate," illegally raking the mollusks from beds owned by others. Then, switching sides, he became a member of the fisheries police, enforcing the law instead of breaking it. His jobs as a sailor took him around the world, and he spent a lot of time on the South Pacific islands. He participated in the Alaska gold rush, then wrote about it in *The Call of the Wild*, an instant best-seller, as was *The Sea-Wolf*. London had little formal education, and his various jobs required muscle more than intellect. He craved unusual experiences, such as living in the worst slums of London for months. Once he even did jail time for vagrancy.

Born in San Francisco, Jack finally settled down on his 130-acre ranch near Glen Ellen and tried running an experimental farm. He strove to live on a grand scale and began building a vast twenty-six-room mansion he called Wolf House. But he never lived in it, as it was torched by an arsonist before he could move in.

The leading characters in Jack London's books were, like himself, heroes of great strength of will who battled their fates with all their powers of mind and muscle. London died at his ranch on November 22, 1916, at only thirty years old. Some claim it was suicide. It seems that his spirit restlessly continues his search for adventure whenever he chooses to appear.

A Real Ghost Writer

It is common for the authors of books to give signed copies of their works to friends as gifts, often with nicely personalized inscriptions. It is not so common to find such a volume bearing the signature of the man pictured on the $50 bill—Ulysses S. Grant, Civil War hero and eighteenth president of the United States.

Why a family in Eureka, California, would have been in possession of such a rare treasure makes an interesting story. But even more interesting is the story of how the precious signed inscription was erased—by a ghost.

There was a connection between the town of Eureka and Grant, though it was early in his military career. Captain Ulysses Grant was stationed at Fort Humboldt, on the southern edge to Eureka, from 1853 to 1854. The fort had been established in 1853 to protect the area from the Indian raids and attacks that repeatedly flared up from the 1850s through 1865. During Grant's service there, however, things were quiet. And evidently boring.

It was claimed that Captain Grant, finding life on the isolated Army post to be dreary and uneventful, spent a lot of time in Patrick Ryan's Saloon in Eureka. Grant was known locally as a "four-finger drinker." In those days, a shot of liquor was measured as a tumbler filled to the height of a man's finger width, so four fingers of booze was roughly equivalent to four shots.

Captain Grant resigned from the Army in 1854, though the reason is in dispute. Some say that his commanding officer forced him out because he had been caught drinking on duty. According to Grant, he resigned out of frustration over the lack of action and the limited opportunity for promotion.

Grant's known association with Eureka was viewed as convincing proof that the inscribed volume of his memoirs found in the town was genuine and thus worth a lot of money. The book in question surfaced in an antique shop. The title page was inscribed, "To Patrick Ryan, a good friend from my days at Fort Humboldt," and signed "Ulysses S. Grant."

The new owner quietly consulted a document examiner, who declared the ink and penmanship style appropriate to the era. Delighted, the discoverer of this rare artifact held a small party to display the memoirs to his family and friends.

The book lay open to show off the inscribed title page. As the group gathered around to view it, a sudden bone-chilling, penetrating cold descended on the room. A mist began to take shape, forming a vaguely human outline. As the group watched, mesmerized, an unearthly brilliant light suddenly glowed directly over the book, and the inked inscription and signature faded away completely. People watched, transfixed, as a modern pen appeared to detach itself from a man's pocket, moving to the book and then writing—all by itself—"Fraud! Shame!" in place of the now-vanished Grant autograph. The apparition then evaporated, leaving the group in stunned silence.

"Well, whoever or whatever that was knew its history," commented a history teacher who was present. "What do you mean?" questioned the book's purchaser. "The inscription and signature had to be fakes," was the reply. "Grant had lost all his money in a bad business deal. He knew he was dying of cancer and wanted to provide his beloved wife with enough money to live comfortably. He drove himself to spend his final months writing his memoirs, hoping that they would sell well and provide for his widow. He did-n't live to see the book published. It did become a best-seller after he died, but he could not have signed this book."

Who, or what, erased the faked handwriting? We'll never know. Would you be interested in buying a genuine first edition of Ulysses Grant's memoirs? Without an author's signature, of course.

The Soldier, the Priest, and the Slave

It is not all that unusual for historic sites and very old buildings to house not just one ghost, but several. Such seems to be the case with the restored and reconstructed buildings of Fort Ross.

The fort stands atop a cliff above a small cove on the Pacific, about one hundred miles north of San Francisco. Originally built in 1812, it represents the southernmost extent of Russian expansion from Alaska into lands claimed by Spain. Now a state historic park, Fort Ross is a popular tourist attraction. And it is home to at least three ghosts.

Fort Ross was short for Fort Rossiya (Russia), and the post stood at the edge of Russian colonial expansion. Over several centuries, Russian power had been extended eastward from Moscow all the way across Siberia to the Pacific Ocean. Russian traders, soldiers, and priests then had crossed the Bering Strait and claimed Alaska for his imperial majesty the tsar. They then began moving down the coast toward Spanish California. The Spanish objected to this intrusion into their territory, and the Russians finally abandoned Fort Ross in 1841, leaving behind fifty-nine log buildings inside a fourteen-foot-high stockade—and three ghosts.

On a typically foggy day, visiting Fort Ross can be a somewhat eerie experience. From the rocky shoreline at the base of the cliff come the hoarse barks of hundreds of California sea lions, which gather on the rocks to rest from their fishing efforts. The fog swirls about the rather crude-looking log structures, and the pale gray light can play tricks on the eyes. Was that a figure moving through the mist or only one's imagination?

Once a visiting family from San Francisco stopped at the fort's ticket booth on their way out. They wished to compliment the park's superintendent on adding to the realism by stationing a man dressed as a Russian soldier at the officers' barracks. "He looked so perfect," they enthused, "wearing a long, heavy wool overcoat and fur hat and carrying a huge old-fashioned musket." "But we don't have any guides or guards in costume," was the reply. "But he saluted us!" said the disbelieving family. The park employee could only shake his head.

Another commonly seen ghost is that of an Orthodox priest who shows up, not too surprisingly, in the Russian Orthodox Chapel. He never appears when live priests conduct services there on Memorial Day, Fourth of July, and the last Saturday in July, but he has been seen on other Sundays and holy days. The spirit is said to be that of a middle-aged man with a long, full beard, wearing elaborately embroidered vestments. Sometimes, observers swear, he can be heard muttering prayers as he kneels before the altar. As soon as he becomes aware of the living, he vanishes.

The third, and perhaps most tragic, ghost is that of a young Indian girl. She has been briefly glimpsed at the commandant's house, where in life, she may have been a kitchen servant. It was not uncommon for Russians at the time to kidnap and enslave local Indians to perform household chores. Pretty, young girls had other uses, too, for Russian men whose wives or girlfriends lived six thousand miles away.

The ghost of the slave girl moves slowly past the great stone fireplace. Her eyes are downcast, and an expression of hopelessness is on her pretty face. In an instant, she is gone. Who was she, and what was her fate? No one knows.

Enjoy your visit to Fort Ross, and watch for "costumed guides" from the spirit world.

The Legend of the Sky Canoe

Tamales Bay, about thirty miles north of San Francisco on the Pacific coast, has a peculiar shape. It looks like a giant string bean—long and narrow, with almost straight, parallel banks. As this trench continues to the southeast, shallow water is replaced by mudflats and then a flat-floored valley. Everyone who has seen it, or even noticed its unusual shape on a map, has expressed some wonder as to what caused Tamales Bay's most unusual configuration. What is the true or most believable explanation depends on one's viewpoint. Geographers have one explanation, but the local Coast

Miwoks have another. Theirs is the more interesting, if you believe in the possibility of UFOs.

To scientists, there is a simple and straightforward reason for why Tamales Bay looks as it does. It has to do with earthquakes. Earthquakes result, they say, when two enormous blocks of the earth's solid crust slide past each other. Except that they don't exactly slide—they can't, as there is too much friction for rock to slide smoothly past rock. The immense tension builds until these blocks suddenly snap apart. We call the jolt an earthquake. The giant crack in the earth along which the movement takes place is called a fault line. The grinding past one another of these rocky blocks pulverizes rock, and the pieces are then easily moved away by running water or ocean waves, producing a valley on land or a bay on the coast. The Coast Miwok tribe has another explanation, however.

Tamales Bay, according to ancient tradition, is the product of a long-ago crash of a titanic UFO, although the Miwoks didn't call it a UFO. Tribal legend has it that huge "sky canoes" visited their home-land, cylindrical objects that looked much like giant versions of the hollowed-out logs the Miwoks used to travel on the ocean. The Miwoks at first assumed that the enormous silver sky canoes belonged to the spirits of the sky, land, and water and were friendly, or at least, benign.

But one beautiful day, one of the sky canoes committed an unforgivable and hostile act—it kidnapped a young woman who had been gathering wild fruits in a large, open meadow. She was returned within an hour, according to legend, but it took her days to recover from a trancelike state. The tribe decided that the sky canoes served evil spirits and must be fought off. But how?

The Miwoks observed that the strange craft landed, or hovered close to the ground, only over large clearings, carefully avoiding the towering redwoods. So they cut through the trunks of several tall trees, securing them in their still-upright position with ropes tied to other trees. A lone young woman was positioned in a clear-ing as bait. Sure enough, a huge sky canoe hovered over her, then slowly descended. The watching Miwoks cut the ropes, causing the great trees to fall against the craft. The sky canoe, or UFO, as we would call it, reacted defensively. Like a great, wounded beast, it powered its way out from under the trees that had fallen across it, surging forth along the ground with flames roaring from it. The escaping craft scraped a huge trench in the earth as it fled in the direction of the ocean. The gigantic gouge it left behind filled with salt water and became Tamales Bay. According to the Miwoks, the mysterious sky canoes ever afterward remained high in the sky, never again venturing to land near the trees.

Yes, agree the Miwoks who believe in the ancient legend, earthquakes do occur along the bay and its interior valley extension, but the scientists are wrong about cause and effect. The quakes occur along the fault line because the scar on Mother Earth left behind by the UFO is an open wound, a weak area where movements focus. And how can we be sure they aren't right?

You Can't Escape

"You can't escape," said a hoarse whisper in her ear. "You can't run away; I'll always find you." The threats were especially scary, coming as they did from a malevolent spirit. Joan Glynn knew from long, painful experience that the ghost spoke the truth, as unfortunate as it was. Despite her precautions, the ghost had tracked her clear across the continent from a small town in New Jersey to her new home in Eureka on California's northern coast. The long-planned, expensive move had been in vain—the ghost had tagged along. The dreaded reason for the cross-country relocation had appeared the very first night in the new home, which Joan had hoped would provide refuge from the tormenting phantom. She had no hope left now of ever achieving freedom from her supernatural stalker.

Most ghosts seem to be associated with specific places or locations. Houses, hotels, restaurants, bars, places of business—all have been said to be haunted. Typically the haunting is limited to a particular room, even an area within a room. The environment itself is haunted, not any particular person. In the case of the Glynns, however, it was a family, not a location, that was the object of the spirit's attentions.

When the Glynns first became aware of the spirit that bedeviled them, they moved across a city and into a new suburb. But the ghost followed, and the family did not get to enjoy a single night's respite from supernatural harassment. The haunting took several different forms. Family members all reported vivid nightmares in which they were being pursued by huge wolves, bears, or lions. Each had awakened, drenched in icy sweat, just as the predator was about to catch them. Another common experience was for the family members to hear threatening voices just as they were about to fall asleep. "You can't escape your fate," the disembodied voices would warn. "You must pay for the sins of your fathers."

One of the more horrible manifestations of the malignant spirits that dogged the Glynn family was the appearance of blood in food or drink they were about to consume. On one memorable occasion, the family was about to toast the birth of another child when suddenly the white wine in their glasses transformed into blood, or so it seemed to them. The blood in their glasses was thick and clotted, and it gave off a foul stench. Shocked, some dropped their glasses to the floor, where, curiously, the contents turned back into wine. A family friend who was present swore that the contents of the wine glasses had never changed to blood, and he couldn't understand the sudden panic among the family as they recoiled from the sight of sparkling wine. Had the family just imagined the blood?

Frequently, family members had terrifying visions—nightmares while fully awake—in which their loved ones were in mortal danger. Every possible calamity was envisioned—car crashes, fatal fires, attacks by armed terrorists, and most disturbingly, suicides. In several instances, the suicides were real. Among the fourteen cousins of Joan's generation, there had been five suicides. Some of the notes they left behind had blamed the "family curse"—but exactly what was the curse?

Joan learned the gruesome origins of the family curse at the bedside of her father as he lay dying of a brain tumor. Her father related the story of the family curse as told to him by his grandfather while the older man was dying. Was what he told her true, or was it merely the product of the cancerous growth?

Joan's great-grandfather had been born in Russia in 1900. As a teenager, he had been forced to join the newly formed Red Army of the Russian Revolution. It was as a young soldier that he had been forced to participate in one of history's most infamous acts—the murder of the former tsar and his whole family. The deposed Tsar Nicholas II, his wife, and their four daughters and only son had been held prisoner by the new Soviet government. Then, fearful that the royal family would become the focus of a counterrevolutionary effort, the government passed down the order to eliminate the whole family.

Joan's father had listened to his grandfather's deathbed confession. The young soldier had been handed a rifle and ordered to be part of a firing squad assembled in the basement of the house where the royal family was held prisoner. On command, her great-grandfather had fired directly into the faces of Russia's last emperor and his family. "The blood—oh, the blood!" he'd told Joan's father. "The blood was everywhere." Far more bullets than were necessary were pumped into the already dead bodies. Her great-grandfather had vomited at the gruesome sight, the memory of which had scarred his soul for life. In his final moment of life, he had screamed, "They've come for me!" and died with a face contorted by fear and terror.

Had the curse of the Russian royals descended down through the generations? Joan is convinced that the sins of the fathers continue for four generations, or so she has been warned by the voices in the night. "You can't run away!" Is it possible that some ghosts are not in our environment, but within ourselves? Joan Glynn thinks so.

Northern

Sierra

THIS VERY LARGE REGION INCLUDES THE HIGH SIERRA FROM YOSEMITE National Park northward to the Oregon border, a distance of more than three hundred miles, and the southern portion of the Cascade Range with Mount Shasta. The physical landscapes range from the world-renowned majesty of Yosemite and Lake Tahoe to the lonely deserts of the northeastern section of the Golden State. This is gold country, where many of the state's fabulous strikes were made, and where ghost towns are believed to host real ghosts along with the tourists.

Among the supernatural denizens of the Northern Sierra are the many ghosts of Bodie, as well as the spirits of Indian warriors, the cannibalized dead of the Donner party, some successful gold prospectors, an irritated art critic, and a glamorous seductress. The legendary bear-man, a mysterious water monster, enchanted rattlesnakes, a possible gateway to hell, and a well-known haunt of UFOs round out this spectacular, specter-filled region.

Beware the Prospector's Ghost

The tiny community of Monoville, on the shores of Mono Lake, has a resident ghost—or at least, it used to have a ghost, for he hasn't been sighted much in recent years. This phantom, those who have encountered it generally agree, is in the form of a grizzled old prospector, wearing a battered cowboy hat and carrying a pick and shovel. The misty apparition appears suddenly out of the gathering gloom at dusk. He is one of a relatively select group of ghosts who speak directly to the living. "Are you looking for gold?" he inquires. "I know where there is a rich strike!" The spirit's eyes glitter with excitement; he beckons his audience to follow him as he trudges off toward the mountains. Sometimes he is accompanied by a phantom mule; more often he is alone.

The ghost is assumed to be that of Heinrik Schmidt, one of three German brothers who supposedly struck gold in the nearby Sierra in the 1850s. The story is that the brothers discovered gold near the headwaters of the Owens River. They told people that they found a thick vein of quartz in which gold nuggets were thickly scattered "like raisins in a pudding." Their story was widely believed because of their habit of paying bills with little lumps of solid gold. But the fabulous luck of the three brothers—Karl, Heinrik, and Adolph—turned very bad indeed one bitter winter. Trapped high in the mountains at their mine by twenty-foot snowdrifts, both Karl and Adolph froze to death. Heinrik survived, but he lost his mind during the ordeal. The legend is that in order to survive, Heinrik killed their mule, disemboweled it, ate the organs, and curled up inside the beast's body cavity to avoid freezing to death. After the first spring thaw, Heinrik stumbled back to Monoville, his clothes crusted with dried blood and his reason gone.

Feverishly, Heinrik tried to sell maps purporting to show the location of the brothers' fabled mine. He would approach strangers on the street and in saloons, trying hard to convince them of the wealth that awaited them at his mine. "Well, why don't you go back and work the mine yourself?" he was asked. "Oh, I dare not go back alone," he would reply. "I didn't have the strength to bury my dear dead brothers. Their spirits may be angry with me for that."

After Heinrik's death, it is claimed that his ghost made regular appearances in the neighborhood, still trying to sell his treasure maps or persuade people to "partner up" and accompany him back to his mine. Should his ghost invite you to follow him back to his gold strike, be cautious. The ghosts of his brothers Karl and Adolph may still be upset that their unburied bodies became food for wolves and vultures.

The Ghost Town's Ghosts

An English teacher would have fun with the term "ghost town." Does it mean the ghost of a town or a town inhabited by ghosts? Actually, it would make sense that the ghost of a town—that is, a collection of abandoned buildings—would be also a town inhabited by ghosts. Bodie, one of California's most famous ghost towns, fits both interpretations, as the long-abandoned old mining town is said to host a remarkable collection of ghosts.

Bodie is popular with tourists for two reasons—its location near beautiful Yosemite National Park and its assortment of colorful spirits. A mile and a half above sea level in the Sierra, the town was named after William Body, a miner who struck gold there in 1859. His spirit apparently is one of the many ghosts who seem to hang out in Bodie. As with many other mining towns, Bodie's fortunes rose and fell repeatedly as mines opened, prospered, were played out by vigorous mining, ran out of gold, were abandoned, and then later reopened as the price of gold and better mining techniques allowed. As miners quickly discovered, the best place to look for gold is near where it has been found before, so mines opened and closed often in the neighborhood. A large strike in 1876 produced a town of twelve thousand miners, would-be miners, storekeepers, saloonkeepers, prostitutes, con men and gunfighters. Frontier mining towns seldom scored high on law and order, and Bodie was one of the wildest. Saloons, brothels, gambling halls, and opium dens lined its streets, which were often the scenes of shootouts and showdowns.

Today the 1,000-acre town of Bodie is a state historic site that is kept in a state of "arrested decay"—that is, the 170 buildings dating back to the 1870s and 1880s are not being restored, but they are prevented from deteriorating further. The park rangers' efforts at keeping visitors from damaging or stealing artifacts get a lot of welcome assistance from a ghost that apparently haunts tourists who walk off with souvenirs. On more than one occasion, local law enforcement officers have received stolen goods returned by mail from repentant thieves. "We are sending back items we took by mistake from Bodie," wrote one family. "Please tell the spirit who has haunted us to leave us alone!" It seems that the phantom of a grizzled old prospector watches over the town and pursues anyone foolish enough to try to lift anything portable from the site. The good news is that this ghost disappears as soon as the article is put back in its proper place, even if only a pebble.

This vengeful guardian spirit also enforces the ban on smoking, which is allowed only in the visitors' parking lot. Nicotine addicts attempting to light up have reported that lit cigarettes or matches were extinguished by unseen hands that wrenched open their mouths and put out the flames on their tongues. No one strikes a match a second time!

Another famous Bodie ghost is that of a Chinese maid who haunts the J. S. Cain House. Short and rather plump, this phantom of a woman who once looked after the children of the household seems to prefer kids to adults. When she materializes around small children, she is all smiles and gives affectionate pats on the head or shoulders. She is very different with adults, however, and sometimes trips them or swats them on the seat. The ghost is especially upset by adults who appear to be too rigid or unfair in disciplining their children. These folks get a painful twist of the ear, so be gentle with children around the Cain House.

Fireplug Annie is one spirit you really don't want to encounter. A notorious denizen of one of Bodie's many brothels, Annie was one tough lady. She was, as they say, "built like a fireplug," having a cylindrical build with no discernible waist or neck. That Annie actually made a living as a prostitute is testimony to just how desperate many miners were, as well as her boldness and determination. The story is that Annie wasn't exactly the shy type; she would walk down the street and grab prospective clients by their coats, more or less bullying them into a transaction. Should you encounter a stout, determined-looking woman in old-fashioned dress approaching you in Bodie, it would be best to move quickly in the opposite direction.

Oh, and don't hang around Bodie at dusk. That's when the really eccentric ghosts appear! Take the phantom gunslinger, for instance. He allegedly swaggers out of a saloon and deliberately knocks down a passerby, hoping to provoke a gunfight. Don't let yourself be drawn into a fight—he's said to be a crack shot. Not all of Bodie's ghosts are scary or aggressive, however. The Angel of Bodie, the spirit of a three-year-old girl accidentally killed by a swinging miner's pick, is said to sit atop her grave, which is marked by a carved angel, laughing and singing nursery rhymes. Bodie's Mendocino House smells of fine Italian cooking, though no one has occupied it for a century. Enjoy (or avoid) the many ghosts of Bodie.

Dancing Spirits

The dancers—or, rather, the spirits of the dancers—appear to be having a high old time. About 120 in number, they whirl about energetically to the music of a fiddle played by an older man in their midst. Several children beat out the peppy rhythm on pots and pans. It is a wild and joyous dance, with everyone participating, a celebration of achievement and relief at having overcome great obstacles. Then, suddenly, unbounded joy turns to terrified panic as shots ring out. The dancers' bodies jerk as bullets hit; blood flows by the gallon as the dead and dying lie in grotesquely twisted heaps. The massacre is complete. No one survives to tell the tale. Weeks later, another wagon train bound for Oregon comes upon the scene of horror—unburied bodies and burned wagons.

What had happened, and why? The full story emerged from a strange account volunteered by a local Indian.

The Indians in the vicinity had seen wave after wave of whites crossing their territory in trains of covered wagons, heading west-northwest toward the Willamette Valley in Oregon. The good news, in the Indian view, was that apparently the whites had no intention of staying in this section of northwestern California. The bad news was that the livestock accompanying the increasingly large and more frequent wagon trains passing through was eating up the grass on which the Indians' game normally fed. Their meat supply was being diminished by the grazing of the whites' horses, mules, and cattle. Resentment among the local tribes was building toward an explosive climax.

Pity the westward-bound pioneers in the 1850s, heading for the lush Willamette Valley. One popular trail to their destination took them from Salt Lake City across the Great Salt Lake Desert and northern Nevada; along the way, the wagons encountered many minor mountain ranges, all running north-south at right angles to their journey. The wagons had to surmount many steep grades through a desolate, forbidding land. Finally crossing into California, they passed through a dry valley, then negotiated a pass over yet another mountain. Ahead lay a seeming paradise—the shining waters of what was then known as Goose Lake, in the beautiful and inviting Goose Valley. At last there was plentiful water for man and beast and ample sweet grass for their exhausted animals. Game animals and birds abounded, providing much-needed fresh meat. Paradise indeed!

Spontaneously, the pioneers stopped their wagons. Dismounting, they began to express their joy in an exuberant Spanish dance—the fandango. As reenacted later by the Indians, the pioneers' fandango was a wild celebration of having surmounted the obstacles of a rugged desert. The sight of the white invaders' merry dance was too much for the Indians watching from the mountainside. Were the whites bewitched by the beauty of the Goose Valley? Would they decide to stay permanently? The Indians charged at the wagons, firing their rifles at men, women, and children. The dancers died in the midst of their celebration, and the local landmarks gained their new names of Fandango Valley, Mountain, and Pass.

To this day, some locals report, the spirits of those long-dead pioneers still dance their fandango on misty summer mornings. But now it is a dance of death.

The Indian Paul Revere

Old-timers around Yreka swear that this spirit of a lovely young Indian maiden once made regular appearances along local roadsides. Today, however, she is seldom seen. In her now-rare materializations, she is running, with an irregular stumbling gait typical of someone nearly ready to collapse from exhaustion. "The warriors are coming!" she cries as she pants breathlessly. "They are coming to attack you!"

The very courageous Klamath Peggy was an important person in the history of Yreka, as she single-handedly averted a massacre of whites by enraged Indians.

Yreka grew almost overnight in 1851 when gold was discovered there. You might say that the gold was discovered by a mule. The mule, belonging to Abraham Thompson, was munching so enthusiastically on sweet grass in the fertile valley that its owner noticed it was pulling up the grass by the roots. Clinging to the roots were large flecks of gold. Within weeks, Thompson's Black Gulch Camp had become an incorporated city known as Shasta Butte, later renamed Yreka, an Indian word for "mountain."

The sudden transformation of what had been one man's remote ranch into a rip-roaring mining town caused consternation among the Klamath Indians. For them, the handwriting was on the wall. Suddenly they were outnumbered in their own land. And the newcomers behaved lawlessly. They were crude and arrogant, shot too many game animals, cut down too many trees, and used too much water in their mining operations.

The Klamaths held many discussions over their campfires about what to do. It was not unanimous, but they reached a decision: The warriors would sneak up on Yreka before daybreak. They would attack without mercy and slaughter all the townspeople in their beds, then burn down the whole town.

Some of the Klamaths feared that starting a war with the whites could only end in disaster for themselves. One woman decided to let the whites know of the impending sneak attack. Klamath Peggy, as she came to be known to the whites, ran for twenty miles to Yreka to warn the town of its fate. Much like Paul Revere on his ride at the beginning of the American Revolution, Peggy breathlessly warned of the coming attack.

Awakened by Klamath Peggy, the citizens of Yreka were alert and on guard as the warriors approached. The Klamaths, faced with the whole town's population armed and ready, withdrew without firing a shot. Bloodshed had been averted through the brave action of Klamath Peggy. Fearing retribution, Peggy never returned to her tribe. She stayed in Yreka, living off a pension granted her by the grateful citizens.

But apparently her spirit still runs along the roads on occasion. "The warriors are coming!" she warns. "Prepare to defend yourselves."

Ghost Warriors of the Lava Beds

The spirits of more than sixty Indian warriors move stealthily across the weird landscape of the lava beds. This fantastic jumble of sharp-edged black rocks, cinder cones, hundreds of caves, and underground galleries forms an eerie wasteland, unusable except as a refuge from pursuers. The lava beds were formed by a volcanic flow of molten rock about five thousand years ago. The pitted surface is just a shell over a labyrinth of tubelike caves. When the surface of the molten rock cooled and hardened, the still-liquid lava underneath drained away, leaving cavities in the seemingly solid rock. This nightmare landscape, which will not support any farming or ranching, makes an ideal hideout, as indeed it was during California's last Indian war—the Modoc War of 1873.

The American takeover of California had been hard on the Indians, especially in the north. When a large band of Modocs laid down their arms to make a peace treaty, soldiers commanded by Captain Ben Wright murdered at least a thousand warriors. Wright boasted that he'd made a "permanent treaty" with the dead. When the government decided to relocate the surviving Modocs to a reservation in Oregon, they were ordered to share a reservation with the Klamath Indians, their longtime bitter enemies, and the trouble accelerated. Chief Kientpoos, known as "Captain Jack," led a band of warriors back to their ancestral hunting grounds in the Lost River country; Army general Edward Canby's forces attacked them, with little success. When Captain Jack suggested a truce and a meeting to discuss the Modocs' future, the general accepted. At that parley, Captain Jack shot and killed General Canby, and the Modocs retreated into the lava beds. There, about sixty warriors held off an army of twelve hundred men for five months. California spent half a million dollars and lost eighty-three soldiers in the infamous Modoc War.

In a way, the Modocs were never defeated in battle. The soldiers surrounded the Indians and cut them off from their water supply. Weak from thirst and a lack of food, the Indians gave up. Captain Jack was hanged at Fort Klamath for the murder of General Canby. Those that remained of the tribe were sent to a reservation in Kansas, never again to see their homes, and never again to use the lava beds as a stronghold against the whites.

Visitors to the Lava Beds National Monument can visit one lighted cave, called Mush Pot, or borrow flashlights to explore other caves on their own. Tourists can view the many Indian drawings left on cave walls. Some visitors claim to have seen the wall paintings come to life—or were they just shadows as the flashlight beams moved over the cave? Better stay in a large group, and don't get between a warrior and his water supply.

The Legendary Bear-Man

One of the most recent sightings of the bear-man (or is it a man-bear?) was by a tourist family in Lassen Volcanic National Park. They were the only ones at that particular campsite, as it was early in the season in late June. The roads were open, but deep snow-drifts still covered much of the forest floor, encouraging the family to stay close to the campsite. That turned out to be just as well, given their experiences with the bear that became a man, then turned into a bear again.

Black bears are plentiful in California. An estimated thirty thousand roam the mountain wildernesses of the state. The California grizzly, once common but now extinct, was an impressive animal, much larger, more aggressive, and more dangerous to people than the common black or brown bear. The grizzly is still the official state animal, appearing on the California flag. The local Indian tribes gave bears a prominent place in their folklore and legends. Some tribes, such as the Shasta of the northeastern part of the state, believed that shamans—medicine men and women—could transform into grizzlies. Shamans were thought to possess supernatural powers, which they could use for either good or evil: They could cure illnesses just by blowing tobacco smoke on their patients and putting them in a trance, or they could kill with the same magic.

The most powerful and feared shamans were the grizzly bear doctors. Bear shamans customarily dressed in bearskin robes, sometimes complete with the skull of a bear atop the head. When in a vengeful mood, so it was said, they actually became bears and wreaked havoc among their enemies.

Bears have a well-known habit of rearing up on their hind legs to get a better look at things or simply appear larger and more threatening. This upright stance frequently is followed by a rapid, four-legged charge. Many believe that reported sightings of Sasquatch or Bigfoot actually are quick glimpses of a bear erect on its hind legs.

"Watch out for bears!" was the advice offered by the park ranger who approved the tourist family's camping permit. "They're recently out of hibernation, and they're hungry." And the alert family did spot a bear surveying them from a distance, standing upright and sniffing the air. Realizing that a charge might be imminent, the father took his rifle out of its locked box as the rest of the family began making as much noise as possible by banging pots and pans. The bear charged, and the father fired a shot into the air. Before their amazed eyes, the bear became a man, who turned and ran away. As he ran, he suddenly became a bear again, racing on four legs, which no man could manage at full speed.

Understandably, the family began packing up their gear and shortly abandoned the campsite. They have no doubts about what they witnessed, but plenty of doubt that anyone would believe them. Did they see modern proof of ancient Shasta Indian legends, or did they, in their terror at an encounter with a bear, simply imagine the bear-to-man-to-bear transformations?

The Donner Ghosts

The very thought of cannibalism is horrifying; that people could actually consume other people is a frighteningly uncivilized concept. Though cannibals definitely existed on some of the South Pacific islands, instances of the practice elsewhere have been rare. That is why cases of cannibalism become so infamous and unforgettable—just ask the ghosts of Donner Lake. On second thought, don't get close enough to those ghosts, should you encounter them, to ask questions. They are particularly gruesome apparitions.

The Donner Lake ghosts are said to appear briefly, and only during snowstorms, which makes it difficult to see them at all. Was that a ghost, or was it just a swirl of snow during a near-whiteout, a time of extremely poor visibility in heavy snows driven by gale-force winds? It is just as well for the observer's sanity that the Donner ghosts are glimpsed for only a second or two. These ghosts, whether men, women, or children, are badly mutilated, and always in the same way: Much of the flesh on their arms and legs has been stripped off, exposing those bones, while their heads and chests usually are intact. The search-and-rescue parties who at last reached the survivors of the Donner party, and the accompanying dead, saw clear evidence of cannibalism on the corpses. It seems that the preferred parts of the body to be eaten first were the upper thighs (think about the hams of pigs), followed by the lower legs and then the arms. The Donner ghosts are those of the partly consumed dead, not the survivors. The spirits of the survivors most

likely stay far from the High Sierra, not wishing to be associated with the scene of their desperate struggle to survive.

Only the most unimaginable desperation could drive Americans to the last resort of cannibalism, so strong is the taboo against such an unspeakable act. But the experience of the Donner party is also testimony to the strength of the will to survive.

The group of emigrants bound for the lush farmland of California's Sacramento Valley set out from Illinois in April 1846, hoping to cross the Sierra by early fall and thus avoid the blizzards that close the passes by December. The eighty-seven pioneers were led by brothers George and Jacob Donner, who made a string of really bad judgments along the way. They decided to try a largely unexplored "shortcut" across the Wasatch Mountains of Utah and were slowed down by wandering up one dead-end box canyon after another. The next challenge was crossing the desert west of Salt Lake, and the party arrived at Reno in late fall, totally exhausted. They decided to rest both people and animals in the lush meadows along the Truckee River. This proved to be a fatal error. They got as far as Donner Lake when they were trapped by an early winter storm with snow twenty feet deep. Their cattle wandered off and disappeared in forty-foot-high drifts. By mid-December, the pioneers were eating mice, as well as their leather moccasins, boots, and snowshoe strings.

Then the first man died of starvation and exposure. The other members of the party devoured his body. Then four more died and also were eaten. Both George and Jacob Donner died and became part of the menu of despair and raging hunger. Of the eighty-seven once-hopeful emigrants, only forty-five lived to see Sacramento.

Today I-80 follows the same path the Donner party once took, as does Amtrak's California Zephyr route. Some of those aboard the Zephyr swear they've caught a quick look at the partly skeletonized Donner ghosts, as have drivers on I-80, so keep a sharp eye for them during snowstorms in the Sierra.

Whatever Lola Wants

This is a very interesting ghost, at least for any men who might encounter her. Unlike many ghosts, who do not interact with the living, this ghost seems intent on reaching into the minds of men, especially those blessed with handsome good looks or fat wallets. More than one man swears that he's had an erotic dream soon after seeing this ghost—extremely erotic, if you know what they mean. Interested? You have to visit Grass Valley and perhaps go picnicking in the mountains nearby.

The phantom of Lola Montez is said to appear in Grass Valley, where she had a home, and also in the vicinity of Independence Lake, a favorite scenic retreat of hers. Near Independence Lake is her namesake, the 9,167-foot Mount Lola. Charm and beauty made Lola internationally renowned as an actress, dancer, entertainer, and close friend to the rich and famous. Lola was, to put it politely, an adventuress. She was famous for being famous—or perhaps infamous, for she was a legendary companion to men whose hearts were filled with lust and pockets lined with gold.

The spirit of Lola Montez is very spirited indeed. Her phantom appears as a young woman of the rather robust build favored in her day. She is not encumbered with much clothing as her voluptuous body sways provocatively in a sinuous dance, a broad, inviting smile on her lovely face. Once men see the supernatural Lola perform her trademark spider dance, they'll never forget it. It will permeate their dreams, very sweet dreams, ever afterward.

Born Marie Gilbert in Ireland around 1818 (she never told anyone how old she was), Lola Montez was a name she just made up to seem more exotic. Her first marriage, of several, was to a military man who was posted to India shortly after they wed. There, according to Marie/Lola, she studied Indian mysticism, dance, and erotic arts.

A few husbands later, she lived in Spain, where she studied dance, especially the tarantella, celebrated for its flamboyant energy and sexual suggestiveness. She changed her name to Lola Montez and embarked on a remarkable career of befriending and dazzling a series of wealthy admirers. King Ludwig I of Bavaria was so charmed that he dubbed her Countess of Lanfeld and showered her with expensive gifts. Other wealthy men lined up for private performances of the spider dance.

In 1852, having heard about the California gold rush, Lola decided to dig a little gold herself—out of lucky miners' pockets. She danced in San Francisco theaters, gold camp saloons, and tents pitched next to gold mines. It was customary for miners to show their appreciation of entertainers by tossing a poke, a small leather bag of gold dust, onto the stage.

Lola settled down in Grass Valley with a pet bear, several dogs, and a husband. The story is that the bear bit the husband, who then shot the bear. Lola divorced her husband because, she said, the bear had the kinder personality.

Leaving Grass Valley in 1854, Lola moved to New York City, where she was unsuccessful at reviving her career as a dancer. Having lost her youthful beauty, she died in poverty in 1864. Her spirit seems to have returned to Grass Valley, where she lived during her happiest years. Lola's ghostly smiling face still beckons invitingly to men who attract her. Is she inviting them to watch her spider dance because they are such handsome devils or because they're rich? Never mind, they will fall under her spell. Whatever Lola wants, Lola gets.

The Phantom Art Critic

It started the day they moved into their South Lake Tahoe condo. The couple, whom we'll call the Richardsons, was filled with joyful anticipation, having hunted for months for that perfect vacation-retirement place. They had long vacationed at Lake Tahoe, and now they owned their own snug piece of paradise. If they leaned over the balcony rail, they could even see a bit of the lake, one of the deepest in the world and surely the most beautiful.

The condo was only about ten years old and came furnished—beautifully furnished, in their view. It had been owned by a professor of fine arts at the University of Nevada–Reno. The walls were hung with attractively framed prints and reproductions of famous works of art. The professor, it seemed, had been a big admirer of the French Impressionists and the American artist Winslow Homer. The Richardsons had a few favorites of their own; their tastes were somewhat broader than the professor's, and they planned some new arrangements of prints in the living room.

Although they also were fans of Vincent Van Gogh, the Richardsons decided that the space on the wall occupied by a copy of *Starry Night* was just the place for their own Picasso print, *Three Musicians*. Picasso replaced Van Gogh, but not for long. That same evening, when they returned from dinner at their favorite local restaurant, the couple discovered that the Van Gogh was right back on the wall and their cherished Picasso reproduction was in their brand new trash can. Concerned, they called the building manager. Had anyone been in their condo while they were gone? They were reassured that no one had entered the unit in their absence. What could have happened? *Starry Night* was once again relegated to the closet, replaced by the Picasso print.

That evening, the Richardsons were rudely awakened by a loud crash from the living room. On investigation, they found the Picasso on the floor, its frame and glass shattered. The couple reluctantly concluded that something very strange was going on.

They began inquiring about the previous owner of the condo and soon learned some interesting details. The "Prof," as he liked to be addressed, had never married and had no family. He had been known as a good teacher, if sometimes impatient with students who openly disagreed with his artistic judgments. The Prof was particularly vehement in his disdain for Picasso. He thought the Spanish artist mediocre, with a flair for publicity and self-advertisement. He also condemned Mondrian as a mere designer, not a creative artist. Any artist who achieved fame after about 1920 was on the Prof's "don't hang" list, according to friends.

At his South Lake Tahoe condo, the Prof had a reputation as a good neighbor, despite hosting rather noisy parties. He always invited all the neighbors to his parties, where they had a good time, easily mingling with the Prof's more exotic guests.

The Richardsons' new neighbors also filled them in on the sad story of the Prof's death. Understandably, the real estate agent who sold them the condo had neglected to mention that the Prof had committed suicide there. Recently diagnosed with AIDS, he had been despondent when told that his disease was progressing rapidly and soon would make him a helpless invalid.

Late one night, the Prof turned on all the lights in his condo, presumably in order to view all his favorite works of art as he sat dying of a massive overdose of sleeping pills washed down with a bottle of expensive French champagne. He left instructions that his condo be sold furnished and decorated just as he had left it. Did the Prof intend to remain in his condo as a spirit so that he could continue to enjoy his collection and tasteful furnishings?

Gradually the Richardsons learned the Prof's "rules." Works not acceptable to the resident art critic's standards were mysteriously relocated to the trash can. Family photos, however, were never subjected to the Prof's rigid taste standards. The couple learned to leave any new piece of artwork on the floor, leaning against the wall. If the Prof's spirit found the art agreeable, it was untouched the next morning. If, however, the picture had been turned toward the wall, they would have to try something else.

The Richardsons condo remains a model of good taste—the late Prof's good taste, that is.

The Lake Tahoe Whatsit

Something is living in Lake Tahoe, and it is a fearsome predator. Few have ever seen it; even fewer have lived to talk about it. And those few seldom talk, as they rightly fear being scorned as neurotic drunks or worse. Who'd believe them? Any report of the outlandishly grotesque monster would surely earn them an agonizingly long stay in a padded cell. Whatever it is that lurks in Lake Tahoe's deep waters is so completely different from all other creatures that it is nearly indescribable. One observer simply calls it a "Whatsit."

Several geologists and geographers have devoted their entire careers to trying to figure out exactly how Lake Tahoe came to be. The lake is twenty-two miles long and twelve miles wide, with two-thirds lying in California and the other third in Nevada. While Tahoe's surface area is impressive enough, this is no shallow saucer of a lake. Its average depth is 1,645 feet below the surface, which is more than a mile above sea level. Most geologists agree that the lake was created by a combination of huge cracks or faults in solid rock, the action of glaciers, and—most interesting in trying to understand the origins of the Whatsit—volcanic activity.

The catalog of Lake Tahoe life forms should be short and sweet: trout. Tahoe teems with several varieties of this tasty gamefish—rainbow, cutthroat, golden, and Tahoe. But what preys on the trout, besides the hordes of fishermen, that is? This is where the elusive and mysterious Whatsit comes in.

Lake Tahoe's clear blue waters are famous for being just about as pure as distilled water. But how can that be? What happens to the fish that die in it or the organic debris that ends up in the lake?

The environmental regulations that protect Lake Tahoe from contamination are among the strictest in the world, but face it, some garbage and sewage are going to find their way into the pristine waters. Who, or rather what, cleans up and recycles dead animals and plants? What form of life is the lake's natural cleanup squad, akin to vultures on land and crabs in shallow seas?

Lake Tahoe never freezes, although it gets 125 inches of snow a year, while surrounding mountains can receive between 300 and 500 inches. The top ten or twelve feet of the lake can reach a temperature of 68 degrees in summer, but the deeper water remains at a constant 39 degrees. No warm-blooded animals could survive in those depths. No fish larger than trout has ever been caught in Tahoe.

What could live in very deep, cold water is some primitive animal without a skeleton, cold-blooded, and hungry for any food, living or dead—a Whatsit, in other words. Some people have theorized that the volcanic activity that helped form Lake Tahoe eons ago could have produced unique mutations of living creatures, perhaps creating a freshwater version of some weird sea creatures like octopus or sea cucumbers. Some deep-sea predators are like big, shapeless blobs of jelly. They feed by simply wrapping themselves around their prey and absorbing it. Other odd deep-sea animals project their stomachs out of their mouths, enveloping and digesting their victims with corrosive stomach acids.

A rare eyewitness account was offered—reluctantly and anonymously, for obvious reasons. A group of friends had been drinking heavily and had reached that stage of inebriation when, though exhausted, they couldn't sleep. They decided to "borrow" a rowboat from a lakeside resort and go fishing. It was just daybreak as they paddled out on the lake. One brought his dog, a German shepherd, with them. They hooked a few fish, but as they were reeling them in, they saw a swirl of disturbed water at the surface. Something wrenched the fish off the hook, leaving part of the trout's jaw still attached. It was difficult to see in the faint light of dawn, but it looked as though a large, translucent blob of jelly had stolen their catch. The dog growled deep in its throat, its fur rose along its spine, and it suddenly jumped into the water. It was a good swimmer, so its owner was not alarmed—until, that is, it disappeared in a violent surge of water, a whirlpool of death. The dog was never seen again.

The would-be fishermen have only a horrifying memory of a silent, shapeless, colorless blob that consumed their fish and the dog. Their theory is that the monster lives in very deep water, rising to the surface at night to feed. They don't advise night fishing on Lake Tahoe.

Moving Pictures

Moving pictures, as early films were called, are associated with Southern California, but Northern California apparently does have its own moving pictures—ancient, supernatural ones. A remote wilderness lying between the Nevada border and Yosemite National Park is renowned for its multiple sites of Indian petroglyphs and pictographs, the scientific terms for stone carvings and picture writings. These mysterious artworks can be seen on the granite cliffs of the White Mountains, near Benton, in Chidalgo Canyon, and also near Chalfont.

One of California's most primitive regions, this was a long-term stronghold of the Paiute tribe. Many believe that at least some of the rock art was created by aboriginal people long before the Paiutes took over, and Paiute tradition supports this concerning some petroglyphs. The pictures carved into solid rock sometimes show human figures, along with representations of deer, bears, bighorn sheep, lizards, and snakes. A few are geometrical designs.

Anthropologists think that these pictures were intended to cast magical spells on the Indians' game animals. Showing the hunters chasing deer would, they prayed, become reality, and there would be plenty of meat in the cooking pots. Other pictures had more obscure meanings. What was the significance, for example, of coyotes chasing people? Or of giant rattlesnakes threatening Indian warriors?

The mystery deepened when photography became common in the late nineteenth century. Early non-Indian travelers had expressed uneasy feelings that some of the figures moved slightly when not being watched constantly. Wasn't that bear on all fours before? Now it was shown rearing up on its hind legs. Was the hunter catching up with a deer, whereas before it was well ahead of its pursuer? When people began taking photos of the drawings, it was said that the pictures moved from day to day, the figures changing their relative positions in a kind of slow-motion ballet.

What was going on? The Paiute stoutly denied that they were altering or redrawing the artworks. Most refused to talk about it with outsiders. One elderly shaman, or medicine man, said that the spirit world was communicating with the living via the magical pictures—that, in fact, the pictures were moving when human eyes were focused elsewhere. Yes, he said, the moving pictures were providing advice or giving warnings to the Paiute and anyone else who was watching closely. A series of photos of the same pictographs, taken on different days, reportedly showed definite changes in the art, which the shaman interpreted for the whites. When, for example, the hunter catches and kills his prey, good times are coming. If the rattlesnake suddenly increases in size and strikes at a human, then great danger lies ahead.

Another curiosity in this region is the Indian rock carvings in a rugged area between Benton and Chidalgo Canyon. These truly mysterious markings appear to be carved into solid rock and show the footprints of both small children and adults, intermingled with the deeper tracks of bears, dogs, deer, and coyotes. The Paiutes adamantly deny making these carvings and claim that they were made by "evil little men who crept out from the rocks at night." They were so disturbed by the track marks that they deliberately destroyed many of them during the 1800s.

Do the pictures actually move? See for yourself, and bring your camera. Did that pictograph of a rattlesnake seem to grow since yesterday? Watch your back.

The UFO Boulevard

Old Dusty figures he's seen them all. Some are bright silver, streaking across the sky, reflecting sunlight like a shooting star. Others are flat black, a hole in the sky, blending perfectly with a moonless night. Some are shaped like darts, with long, slender bodies and relatively small, swept-back fins. Others look more like triangles or boomerangs. Still others resemble the now-classic descriptions of flying saucers or giant Frisbees. Sometimes they carry no light whatsoever, though many are rimmed with twinkling lights like a carnival ride or seem to glow with bright, pulsing inner light. Yes, Dusty has seen them all in his six decades of living in a remote wilderness in the northeast corner of California. Some might call them unidentified flying objects, but Dusty calls them "the government-doesn't-want-you-to-know flying objects."

Dusty, who doesn't want to be identified except by his nickname, owns and operates a service station along a particularly remote section of U.S. 395, which traverses some of the loneliest country in the western United States. From the Canadian border to San Bernardino, Route 395 runs as close to north-south as geography permits. Southward from the Oregon border, it crosses a wilderness of forested mountains and desert valleys, veering into Nevada through Reno and Carson City before reentering California for its journey through the Mojave Desert on its way to the Los Angeles area.

Dusty acquired his nickname because travelers stopping for gas and a cold soda often remarked, "Kind of dusty here, isn't it?" Indeed it is dusty and lonely, and Dusty has had plenty of opportunity to observe the sky, both day and night. He's seen, by his estimation, hundreds of UFOs over the decades. They appear so frequently over the stretch of highway between Alturas and Susanville because, Dusty figures, there are few people to observe them or get excited by their unbelievable speed and maneuverability. His theory is that his almost empty part of the world is used for testing experimental aircraft of our own in secret. Dusty laughs at the idea of aliens from outer space checking us out. He claims that the U.S. Air Force and CIA encouraged the "aliens from space" theories to deceive the Cold War-era Soviets, and everyone else, about the successes of American aviation research.

Is it pure coincidence that northwestern California is only minutes of flying time from an enormous piece of Nevada desert between Las Vegas and Tonopah that is controlled by the U.S. military? This land, the size of Switzerland, contains the huge Nellis Air Force Base, bombing range, and nuclear weapons test site. Super-secret aircraft such as the incredibly fast, high-altitude spy plane of the 1950s, the famous U-2, are supposed to have been developed and tested at Nellis. Dusty is of the opinion, and he is not alone, that the U.S. government may have started, or at least fostered, rumors of alien spacecraft piloted by weird, unearthly life forms to distract the Russians from realizing just how far ahead we were in developing exotic aircraft.

Stealth bombers and vertical-takeoff jet fighters no longer are secret. Their prototypes, flashing through the night skies of the past four decades, certainly were, though, and who knows what star-tling new experimental craft are the latest to cruise the remote desert's skies.

Is Dusty right? Is the whole UFO thing just a cover story made up and spread by the Air Force and CIA? Or was it a convenient and timely distraction for exactly what some assumed—visits from outer space that happened to coincide with great strides in Ameri-can research and development of aircraft and spacecraft?

Perhaps we'll never be sure, so keep an eye on the skies over Route 395—you just might see something truly awesome. Maybe Dusty is right. Or maybe he's not. Are those UFOs coming from Nellis or a far-off galaxy? Maybe 395 should be renamed the UFO Boulevard.

How to Kill a Witch

The tiny community of Rough and Ready was founded, not surpris-ingly, by a group of miners who called themselves the Rough and Ready Boys—ready for anything and anyone. Anyone except a witch, that is. A local family's tradition holds that one of their ancestors, a gold miner who arrived in Rough and Ready around 1850, actually met a witch. Not just any witch, but a shape-shifting one. The miner not only met her, but also outwitted and killed her—and as everyone knows, it's not easy to kill a witch.

Now, the miners of Rough and Ready were a highly independ-ent group. At the urging of a barmaid named Hecate, known as Kate, they held a mass meeting in a saloon to protest the federal taxes on gold mining. None liked to pay taxes, so the miners declared the "free and sovereign state of Rough and Ready." They drew up a constitution prohibiting any taxes and declared their secession from the Union. Kate was elected "queen of the damned," and few could have known just how appropriate that title was.

Queen Kate took in a boarder, one Jack White, who eventually proved to be her killer. Jack was a handsome man, and Kate was a nubile young woman, so they paired up. Jack was quite happy with this arrangement but began to notice something odd about Kate. If he would happen to wake in the middle of the night, Kate was nowhere to be found. What was she up to? Jack decided one night to pretend he was sound asleep and watch her.

What Jack witnessed was astounding and not just a little frightening. Hecate reached behind her neck, grabbed her thick black hair, and yanked off her skin, shedding it like a huge snake. Stepping out of her skin was a coal-black mountain lion, which tossed the discarded skin under the bed and slunk out the door. Jack followed the big cat to a clearing in the woods, where a satanic ceremony was under way. The sleek mountain lion participated in horrific rituals around a roaring campfire. Jack prudently sneaked away home, where he fell into a troubled sleep.

The next day, Kate was her usual self, back in her woman skin. That evening, Jack again pretended to be sound asleep as Kate once more slipped out of her skin and ran off to her nightly orgy of devil worship. Now Jack figured that sooner or later, he would be targeted as a human sacrifice. He would not be able to fight off the mountain lion version of Kate. What to do?

In a flash of inspiration, Jack took the temporarily abandoned skin and rubbed the inside with salt—lots of it. He then pretended to be asleep when the big cat returned. It slipped back into its woman skin, and then writhed in agony as the salt stung it. Hecate the witch died on the floor at dawn, and Jack went on to live a long, witch-free life.

Don't Tread on Me

"Don't tread on me," as students of American history will recognize, was the motto featured on a flag popular with revolutionary-minded patriots around 1776. The flag showed a coiled rattlesnake above the motto. The flag's meaning was clear: Don't mess with the American colonials, or they'll strike back with deadly effect. The rattlesnake warns of danger by shaking the rattles on its tail; ignore the warning at your peril.

The legend of Indian Joe is that one man somehow established a mystical bond with rattlesnakes and used these fearsome creatures to obtain justice, at least as he defined justice. Teaching rattlers to become fanged executioners meant modifying their behavior. These snakes use their rattles to avoid confrontations with creatures too big to eat and large enough to trample them. Indian Joe is said to have gotten inside their brains and taught them not to rattle when on a death mission for him.

Indian Joe lived in what is now Yosemite National Park. He was born about 150 years ago, the son of a Native American woman and an English trapper and hunter. The unkind term "half-breed" was applied to Joe, and he didn't have an easy childhood. Both parents taught him what they knew about living nature—plants, animals, and all of creation—and Joe grew up playing more with animals than with other children, who scorned and mocked him. He began to plot revenge. His mother's brother, a well-known shaman, taught Joe how to enter the minds of game animals—deer, rabbits, and elk—and hypnotize them. Under Joe's mental control, the creatures would be drawn to where he hid and readied to kill them for the cooking pot. The mesmerized animals would voluntarily enter his traps, and Joe, in return, would respectfully offer prayers for their new existence in the spirit world. At least, that was the Indian belief at the time.

Despite his mastery of Indian lore under his uncle's tutelage, Joe was still rejected as an outcast by his contemporaries. He resented this treatment and was especially enraged when the tribe scorned his mother as well.

If, Joe reasoned, he could connect with the souls of rabbits and deer and bend them to his will, maybe he could also work this magic with rattlesnakes. Rattlers played an important role in local Indian mythology. They could deliver sudden death through their fangs. Although they struck their food, mostly small rodents, in swift silence, they gave fair warning of their presence to all creatures too big to eat. Joe set about persuading rattlers to approach people and kill in silence at his command. Some believe that he mixed tobacco with weeds containing hallucinatory drugs, burned them, and blew the smoke at the rattlers to achieve his dominance over them. Joe is said to have admitted to using this technique, and he promised to leave the formula behind before he died. It was even claimed that Joe captured baby rattlers and raised them in covered baskets, training them to be his assassination squad.

The first victim of Joe's vengeance was a neighbor woman who spread vicious gossip about his mother. A large rattler crept into her bed one night, and she was dead within minutes. A young man, a rival of Joe's for the attention of a lovely young lady, stooped to pick wildflowers for his girl. A rattler sprang up from a clump of flowers and sank its fangs into his throat. The venom reached his brain and killed him before he could cry out.

One by one, anyone who angered Indian Joe was killed by his reptile minions. Word spread throughout the mountains that Joe had entered the minds of rattlesnakes, which would kill at his command, ruthlessly and uncharacteristically silently.

When Joe reached old age, true to his word, he painstakingly engraved his instructions for hypnotizing rattlers and commanding their actions on a slab of granite. The stone was to be placed over his grave in a secret location known only to his family. This was done, and Joe's formula for converting rattlesnakes into assassins is still there. But there is one problem—Joe's grave and gravestone are deep underwater. Joe's home was in the Hetch Hetchy Valley. The city of San Francisco spent twenty years building O'Shaughnessy Dam across the mouth of the valley to create a huge reservoir for its water supply. Joe's tombstone is said to have featured a coiled rattler with the motto "Don't tread on me!" along with his description of how to enter the minds of rattlers and make them do your bidding. Interested? Too bad scuba diving is not permitted in Hetch Hetchy Reservoir.

The Ghosts of Jamestown

Considering that it was named for a failure, the gold-mining town of Jamestown turned out to be a pretty lucky place for at least some miners. One local mine alone, the Humbug, yielded more than $4 million worth of gold, and that was back when $1 was a decent day's wage.

Jamestown was named for Colonel George James, a lawyer from San Francisco who arrived there in 1848 and opened the first mine. Though James looked hard, he never found any gold. He quarreled with his neighbors, mostly about alcoholic beverages. James didn't drink and was not pleased when his neighbors did, to noisy excess. He wanted a dry town but was hopelessly outvoted—everyone else was enthusiastically wet. James packed up and returned to San Francisco a bitterly disappointed man. The day after he left Jamestown, another man who'd taken over George James's claim found a gold nugget the size of a hen's egg. The lesson was clear to all: Nondrinkers lacked the luck in finding gold. The rest of

Jamestown's miners pledged to drink up in order to improve their luck. That habit was indeed lucky, at least for saloon owners and bartenders.

It is said that the ghost of George James still shows up now and then to admonish fools not to drink. Just as in 1848, most people ignore unlucky George James and go right on having a drink or two. Don't worry, James's ghost fades away as that first drink is downed, and the drinkers frequently get lucky. Not just in finding gold, either.

George James is not the only ghost to show up in Jamestown, which was known to early miners as Jimtown. The town is a popular attraction for tourists, with its fine collection of balconied old buildings and covered sidewalks. Many visitors have an odd feeling that they've been there before. This may be because the town has served as a background for scenes in movies, including *High Noon* and *Butch Cassidy and the Sundance Kid*. The town's historic business district now features galleries, boutiques, and of course, saloons in which to improve one's luck. A few other ghosts add to Jamestown's charm.

The most frequently seen phantom is said to be that of an attractive woman simply known as Flo, as no one knows her real name. Flo makes her cameo appearances at the historic National Hotel, built in 1859. The National has only nine bedrooms, so visitors have a good chance of meeting Flo. She also has been known to appear in the hotel's restaurant and bar, where she impresses patrons by walking right through walls. Many bar customers have seen Flo walk through walls after they've finished their fourth drink.

Flo is a somewhat mischievous spirit. She sometimes packs up guests' luggage while they are downstairs in the restaurant, causing them to have to unpack again before bedtime. Some hotel guests claim that lights flicker on and off and doors suddenly slam shut as Flo makes her daily rounds of guest rooms, making beds and sweeping floors.

There are those who swear that Flo once stood in for a bartender who was taken ill. She allegedly poured generous drinks and joked with her customers, reminding them that having a stiff drink would drive away the ghost of George James. So ignore the disapproving stare of the ghost of George James, and drink up. Flo just might glide by and walk through the wall for you. By the way, if you are one of the few tourists who don't drink at all, you may be shadowed everywhere by James's ghost. He'll follow you around out of sheer admiration and means no harm. Still, it can be a little unnerving to acquire a permanent shadow like that while visiting, so to get James's spirit to go elsewhere, you only have to have a drink. Drink up!

Hell's Back Door

Everyone knows that abandoned mines are very dangerous places. Even tourists can figure that out. To start with, you risk falling into a hole, which could be a very deep one. Then, too, rattlesnakes retreat into the shade and relative cool of mine tunnels during the heat of the day, as do scorpions. Rotted support timbers can give way suddenly, causing a roof to collapse. Old wooden ladders are likely to break under the stress of being used for the first time in decades, trapping the unwary underground.

So there are plenty of good reasons to stay well away from the old gold or silver mines that dot the area between the Nevada border and the high peaks of the Sierra in the vicinity of Mono Lake. Add a supernatural threat, and you have the mother of all dangerous places.

The exact location of Hell's Back Door will not be revealed. Enough innocents and reckless adventurers have died already. The mine entrance is protected by a chain-link fence—common practice around old tunnel mouths visible from the highway. Coyotes, however, have burrowed under the fence, attracted by the odor of decaying flesh, so the fence doesn't keep out determined scavengers—or determined people.

No one knows how the old mine known as Hell's Back Door got its name. Did the early prospectors who first dug there for gold assign the name, or did later generations of law officers and bad guys call it that in recognition of its evil reputation?

It seems that Hell's Back Door mine probably produced more human bones than gold. Local legend has it that among the mine's first human victims were a couple of stagecoach robbers who apparently sought refuge in the dark hole while fleeing from a pursuing posse. Years later, their remains were discovered, along with the stolen strongbox, by a cowboy seeking shelter from a spring snowstorm. The box was still filled with gold nuggets. There was no way to know how the robbers had met their death, not that anyone cared.

A more recent tragedy, back in the 1930s, provided some clues about how Hell's Back Door might have earned its satanic nickname. A highway patrolman making his rounds spotted a coyote trying to drag a human arm out of the mouth of the mine. Now, coyotes, unlike mountain lions or bears, are not capable of killing adult humans. In fact, they tend to stay well clear of people by preference. Coyotes will, however, eat fresh corpses of any size. The state patrolman investigated the old mine and discovered two bodies. These two unfortunates probably had been looking for relics of the long-disappeared miners, such as discarded equipment or old bottles, which can bring money in antique markets. Although there was a long list of possible causes of death, such as rattlesnakes, the bodies were cherry red in appearance. Only one cause of death produces bright red flesh in its victims—carbon monoxide poisoning. People who die in poorly ventilated homes using kerosene heaters look that way also.

With carbon monoxide poisoning determined to be the cause of death, where was the unvented fire that produced the deadly gas? There was no sign of a campfire in or near the mine tunnel. It was a mystery. Local Indian lore suggested a supernatural cause. The Indians had believed that the white man's digging underground was the ultimate folly, that tunneling into the ground would free the evil spirits trapped there at the beginning of time. Just as European-Americans believed that the Devil's domain lay beneath their feet in a fiery hell, Native Americans believed in an underground world of hostile spirits who danced around eternal fires. It was simple, said the Indians; the carbon monoxide had come from the fires of hell. And hell was deep inside the mine. All deep mines therefore were doorways to hell, so one should never venture into a mine and thus come closer to the eternal fires attended by evil spirits.

So stay out of abandoned mines. If the rattlesnakes don't get you, the fumes of satanic fires will.

I Should've Stayed in California

"I should've stayed in California," this ghost used to lament as he stared into the whiskey glass that didn't seem to ever leave his hand. "I struck it rich here and never should have left," he would tell anyone kind enough to buy him a drink. This phantom really liked his drink, and he would down a whole lot more than one in an evening of telling stories. Telling stories was a pleasure—something that he did very well. Although this spirit hasn't been spotted much recently, some folks in Angels Camp swear they've met him in the bars of the old Hotel Angel or the Calaveras Hotel. It's too bad that this ghost now makes only brief, rare appearances, as his stories about life in the Sierra gold camps of a century and a half ago were really interesting. He is assumed to be the ghost of the writer Bret Harte, once almost as famous as his onetime drinking companion and buddy Mark Twain.

By an interesting coincidence, both Bret Harte and Mark Twain first rose to fame as writers on the basis of stories set in gold-mining towns like Angels Camp. They even may have first heard the tales on which they based their writings in the local saloons.

"Yes, I struck it rich here," the ghost supposedly would tell his avid listeners. "Did you strike gold?" was an obvious question from his new friends as they bought him another drink. "No, I didn't actually find gold, but I found some great characters among the miners for my stories," he would reply. Indeed, Bret Harte did find literary gold in the Sierra, for he is credited with starting an entire genre of American fiction—the realistic, if dramatized, tales of rip-roaring mining towns with their assortment of highly independent, tradition-smashing, hard-drinking miners, cowboys, bartenders, prostitutes, sheriffs, and bad guys. The tales of the saints and sinners of the frontier made for great reading, and half the Wild West movies you've seen likely reflected the Bret Harte style of story-telling.

Born in Albany, New York, in 1836, Bret Harte arrived in California around 1856, looking for adventure. He worked as a school-teacher and newspaperman, setting type as well as reporting on local events. Like most writers, he needed to keep his day job while building his reputation as an author, so Bret earned a living as secretary of the San Francisco Mint. He and Mark Twain also wrote for the city's newspapers.

After his short stories made him nationally famous, Bret moved to Boston in 1871, never to return to California. Except in spirit, that is. His literary career sank like a stone in a pond after leaving the Golden State. He and Mark Twain collaborated on a play, which was a flop. He went back to government jobs, serving as an overseas consul in Germany and England. He died a poverty-stricken drunk in England in 1902. His ghost was right: He really should've stayed in California. Be sure to buy Harte's spirit a drink if you come across him in a saloon—his stories will more than repay you.

Bibliography

Books

Ainsworth, Edward. *Beckoning Desert*. Englewood Cliffs, NJ: Prentice Hall, 1962.

American Automobile Association. *Southern California and Las Vegas*. Heathrow, FL: AAA Publishing, 2007.

Ault, Philip. *How to Live in California*. New York: Dodd, Mead, 1961.

Beckley, Timothy. *The UFO Silencers*. New Brunswick, NJ: Inner Light, 1990.

Botkin, B. A., ed. *A Treasury of American Folklore*. New York: Crown Publishers, 1944.

Clark, Jerome. *Unexplained!* Canton, MI: Visible Ink Press, 1999.

Coleman, Loren. *Mysterious America*. London: Faber and Faber, 1983.

Crow, John. *California as a Place to Live*. New York: Scribner's, 1953.

Dorson, Richard. *American Folklore*. Chicago: University of Chicago Press, 1959.

Drury, Aubrey. *California: An Intimate Guide*. New York: Harper, 1947.

Federal Writers Project. *California: A Guide to the Golden State*. Rev. ed. New York: Hastings House, 1967.

Guiley, Rosemary. *The Encyclopedia of Ghosts and Spirits*. New York: Facts on File, 1992.

Harper, Charles. *Haunted Houses: Tales of the Supernatural*. Philadelphia: J. B. Lippincott, 1930.

Hauck, Dennis William. *Haunted Places: The National Directory*. New York: Penguin Putnam, 2002.

Jacobson, Dan. *No Further West: California Revisited*. New York: MacMillan, 1959.

Krantz, Les. *America by the Numbers: Facts and Figures from the Weighty to the Way-Out*. Boston: Houghton Mifflin, 1993.

Lewis, Oscar. *High Sierra Country*. San Francisco: Duell, Sloan, 1955.

Mack, John. *Abduction: Human Encounters with Aliens*. New York: Scribner's, 1994.

Myers, Arthur. *The Ghostly Register*. New York: McGraw-Hill, Contemporary Books, 1986.

Pickering, David. *Casell Dictionary of Superstitions*. London: Casell, 1995.

Skinner, Charles. *American Myths and Legends*. Detroit: Gale Research Co., 1974.

Stein, George, ed. *The Encyclopedia of the Paranormal*. Buffalo, NY: Prometheus, 1996.

Taylor, Troy. *The Haunting of America: Ghosts and Legends from America's Past*. Alton, IL: White Chapel Productions, 2001.

Thompson, C. J. S. *The Mystery and Lore of Apparitions*. London: Harold Shaylor, 1930.

Online Sources

www.californiaghosts.com
www.legendsofamerican.com/Caghostlylegends
www.worldreviewer.com

Acknowledgments

THIS IS MY EIGHTH BOOK WRITTEN UNDER THE SKILLFUL GUIDANCE AND friendly encouragement of my editor, Kyle Weaver. I appreciate his counsel and confidence in me. Kyle's assistant, Brett Keener, capably piloted the manuscript through the production process with sensitivity and precision. The imaginative and evocative illustrations are the creative work of a very talented artist, Heather Adel Wiggins.

I wish to thank the helpful staff of the California Travel and Tourism Commission at Sacramento, as well as the folks at the various county and municipal tourism bureaus who were so generous with their time and advice. The friendly professionals at Pitman Library, the Gloucester County Library, and Rowan University's Campbell Library provided invaluable help. Herb Richardson of Richardson Books tracked down the "oldies but goodies" volumes that I needed. My darling wife, Diane, was my copilot in navigating the Internet; she also accompanied me on our delightful fieldwork in that most beautiful of states, California. Thanks again, my sweetheart.

About the Author

CHARLES A. STANSFIELD JR. TAUGHT GEOGRAPHY AT ROWAN UNIVERSITY for forty-one years and published fifteen textbooks on cultural and regional geography. In the course of his research, he realized that stories of ghosts and other strange phenomena reflect the history, culture, economy, and even physical geography of a region. He is the author of *Haunted Southern California, Haunted Jersey Shore, Haunted Maine, Haunted Ohio, Haunted Vermont,* and coauthor with Patricia A. Martinelli of *Haunted New Jersey.*

Other Titles in the
Haunted Series